Submit

Sonnet is the pseudonym of a businesswoman based in London and New York.

Submit

a memoir by Sonnet

CORONET

First published in Great Britain in 2024 by Coronet
An imprint of Hodder & Stoughton Limited
An Hachette UK company

1

A CIP catalogue record for this title is available from the British Library

Hardback ISBN 9781399729499
ebook ISBN 9781399729512

Typeset in Monotype Sabon MT by Manipal Technologies Limited

Printed and bound in Great Britain by Clays Ltd, Elcograf S.p.A.

Hodder & Stoughton policy is to use papers that are natural, renewable and recyclable products and made from wood grown in sustainable forests. The logging and manufacturing processes are expected to conform to the environmental regulations of the country of origin.

Hodder & Stoughton Limited
Carmelite House
50 Victoria Embankment
London EC4Y 0DZ

www.hodder.co.uk

For Max, here's to many, many more adventures.
I love you.

Contents

NOTE ON LANGUAGE:
My cunt is my powerful, monosyllabic, Anglo-Saxon cunt. It is just not a pussy or vagina, sorry.

TRIGGER WARNING:
Actual subjugation is completely opposite to elective submissive surrender, and does not inhabit the same universe psychologically as the kinks this book will describe, but please do be aware that there are scenes depicted of consensual physical pain being caused to a woman.

Introduction

'Th' expense of spirit in a waste of shame
Is lust in action; and till action, lust
Is perjured, murd'rous, bloody, full of blame,
Savage, extreme, rude, cruel, not to trust . . .'

– From Sonnet 129, William Shakespeare

'Trust me, it's paradise. This is where the hungry come to feed. For mine is the generation that travels the globe and searches for something we haven't tried before. So never refuse an invitation, never resist the unfamiliar, never fail to be polite and never outstay the welcome. Just keep your mind open and suck in the experience. And if it hurts, you know what? It's probably worth it.'

– *The Beach*, Alex Garland

I can remember my earliest submissive fantasies, not that I knew that's what they were back then. My religious mother would read Bible stories to us before bed. When she switched off the lights, I would start picturing myself on an ark surrounded by animals, or living it up in the belly of a whale, but my brain would immediately take me to the – many – places of humiliation and pain I had heard about. I would imagine myself into a desert landscape, being stoned by the elders for a sin my eight-year-old brain certainly couldn't understand, or being dressed in sackcloth and ashes and paraded through dusty streets. Or forced into servitude by a Babylonian king, then locked in prison with a lion. Even that first fundamental story of castigation would go round my head, as I saw myself naked, eating a delicious apple and receiving the ultimate and shameful punishment: banishment from Eden for ever. Lying in bed, I couldn't stop viscerally imagining myself into these situations. I didn't know why I kept doing it, and I had a strong sense that I was not supposed to be thinking this way, and that if my parents could somehow see inside my brain they would be horrified. I knew this was not what these stories were *for*, even if I couldn't really explain what it was I was doing with them.

Soon my daydream repertoire expanded to include events imagined from books and films. I read *The Little Princess* and imagined myself stripped of my fine clothes and forced to live as a servant in a garret. I pictured myself as a chimney sweep in *The Water Babies*, or as Bonnie and Sylvia at the brutal mercy of Miss Slighcarp in *The Wolves of Willoughby Chase*. In a Dickens phase, I fancied myself as an orphaned Oliver or David Copperfield, destined for the workhouse. I loved the asylum in *Return to Oz*, and even went through a brief period of imagining myself helplessly bound to a wheelchair like Pollyanna or Colin in *The Secret Garden*.

My primary school had a chilly outdoor pool with rudimentary wooden changing rooms, and I spent hours of childhood night-times vividly imagining variations on the theme of being plunged into an ice-cold pool by the teacher, in front of all my classmates, as punishment for some crime. My Sunday school had strict lessons about right and wrong, and my night-time brain loved to turn over the punishments that would befall me if I fell afoul of the rules.

I didn't think about whether I did or didn't want these things to actually happen. I never thought about them during school or ballet lessons or when I was playing with my friends. They were just stories my brain wanted to tell me at night, and I had no choice but to listen. To myself, I called them 'bad daydreams'; I had instinctive shame around them and knew not to tell anyone about them. I wonder, now, where that shame came from – no baby is born with a sense of shame. Some shame is taught to us deliberately: around our naked bodies, for example, as once we are past the age of about five, we are told it is just not OK to throw off our clothes in public; and around most bodily functions, which we are taught must only be dealt with in private. But in my case, I wonder if it was simply that I knew I wasn't doing what I was told, and I knew that was wrong. When I couldn't sleep, mum told me to imagine 'happy things' – running on a beach, turning pirouettes on a stage, building a snowman – and when I didn't, preferring my other 'bad daydreams', I was therefore disobeying her. It was the early eighties, and my parents would not have heard of the concept of a child psychologist, but I wonder if I had seen one at the time, would I have been misdiagnosed with intrusive thoughts or OCD?

I discovered masturbation physically. The water felt nice moving across me in the bath, and I realised I could recreate the feeling with my hands. Some children find it naturally like this; others hear about it and consciously decide to give it a go. When I learned about it from friends – certainly not from my parents – it was a revelation: 'Oh, *that's* what that is.'

It wasn't long before the internal storytelling mingled with my tentative physical explorations. As a teenager, I kept trying to get myself off to thoughts of Johnny Depp or Brad Pitt, and romance and beaches and kissing, as *Just Seventeen* and *Mizz* magazines implied I should. These attempts did work, but somehow a humiliating or violent subplot would sneak in against my best mental efforts. My version of *Four Weddings and a Funeral* would inexplicably end with Hugh Grant leading me naked through the rain by a lead. If I was Buffy, the vampires would vanquish me and drink all my blood. I would come, and immediately think, *What is wrong with me?* I would not have been able to articulate that feeling as sexual shame, but of course that's what it was.

As a teenager, I launched myself into discovering the kind of sex life we gossiped about in the common room and at sleepovers. I kissed lots of boys and lost my virginity to a special one. I was joyful and curious about sex, and genuinely loved discovering how bodies worked and felt. I talked to my friends about sex and relationships all the time, but it would not have occurred to me to mention anything about what secretly played out in my head, or indeed that there could ever be a connection between my imaginary stories and real life. The fantasies sometimes popped up during sex; I would desperately push them out of my mind, trying to focus on the task at hand, feeling mortified that a vision of my sweet teenage boyfriend stamping his foot onto my face had wormed its way in unbidden – and how extra wet that would make me.

In my final year of university, my boyfriend – a Jude Law lookalike a few years older than me, a Cambridge graduate on a city traineeship, firmly the upper end of middle class, and one of those competent, good guys who would help old ladies, give money to charity, and have definite thoughts on how to barbecue steak – asked me what my fantasies were. It was the first time anyone had asked me that. I blushed bright red, clammed up and refused to tell him, which resulted in him taking offence and us not fucking for weeks. I'd lie awake as he snored with his back to me, fingering myself. The shame at what secretly turned me on, and the fact that I could never tell someone like him, would become arousing in itself, in a meta narrative of delicious imaginary humiliation.

Through my twenties and the pre-crash noughties, I had fun – I had threesomes (always two girls, one guy), and went to heteronormative sex parties where everyone dressed like they were at a gallery opening and the men never touched each other. I shagged colleagues ill-advisedly on work trips and went home with people I met in bars. But still my inner submissive fantasy life remained just that.

Then I met Max. His boyish, almost cherubic looks, and chilled surfer-boarder-climber calm belied an imagination so off-the-chart deviant that I rapidly discovered my reluctant, self-invented BDSM fantasising was not only easy to confess, but actively turned him on. Max's secret talent was the internet. I had always thought of online dating, early social media, forums – the internet in general – as being for geeky introverts who couldn't make friends in real life. Max decided it was a miraculous gateway: one that could bring the storylines that had played so secretly through my mind for twenty years into, if not the cold light of day, the dimly lit reality of night. He found clubs behind secret doors throughout the city; he befriended people on special websites and got us invited to private parties. As our friends began to get married, move to the suburbs and have kids, we went gleefully, secretly, hand in hand down a rabbit hole of kink.

I learned that many other people, like me, were innately aroused by being submissive. Others loved to be submitted to, and accepted that this is just what did it for them. Others were 'switch' – equally aroused by both scenarios depending on the circumstance. I can certainly play-act the dominatrix, and it can be fun, but for me it would never feel *real* in the way that it does when I surrender my body and mind to another person or people. Max certainly got off on the creation of scenarios, on pushing me to do things and seeing how far I would go. And he had a classic geek's love of learning and perfecting a skill: tying shibari, using a flogger, taking photographs and developing his own film (some pictures you just don't want to take to Snappy Snaps). We met people who had definitely spent their 10,000 hours on perfecting accurate caning, or needle play, or erotic hypnosis, and were truly talented artists. I felt honoured to become one of their canvases.

I learned that in real life, unlike in fantasy, submission is much more about a beautiful symbiotic dialogue with another person or people. I began to understand that it is the opposite of sexual assault, where the victim is, by definition, not consenting to what is happening, or has been coerced, or has had systemic power used against them. When I submitted to dominants in real life, it was an act of total, willing surrender – and it was my active positive submission that turned them on, NOT their taking something without permission or through an abuse of status. It is shame-free.

I loved listening to what the dominants thought. I have never met one who is not extremely kind, thoughtful and about as far from endorsing violence against women as people can be. They have often struggled to reconcile what gets them off in the bedroom (practised with very willing participants) with horrific violence in the outside world, and this can be a source of distress. But they react to a submissive's desire, and they respond sensitively – albeit perhaps brutally – to what they see and feel. To do this, they need vast reserves of attuned empathy. They have to be hugely creative, as they are leading the proceedings, even if you have been very clear in advance about what does it for you and what's OK. I've found kink people have often given so much thought and reflection to their interactions with others that they are significantly more emotionally articulate and evolved than people whose sexual desires are either so 'normal' they've never had to, or so sadly repressed that they can't.

Within the basic idea of 'submission', I learned there was a huge spectrum of ideas to play with. There were a thousand kinds of role play, and every conceivable combination of people, from one-on-one to a vast party of hundreds. My fantasies had always centred around ideas of power and surrender, humiliation and pain. But I began to learn the nuances between them. Humiliation – for me – can be close to exhibitionism. An early discovery of ours was fetish photography. There are many talented photographers out there who want to depict submission, and are always looking for models. The idea of being dropped off by Max on his scooter, at a photographic location, where I would be naked, tied up, forced – maybe manually – into various positions, while someone photographed me, was tinglingly humiliating . . . but also tapped into the massive show-off, attention-loving, vain side of my personality. Opening the door to a man completely naked, or being stripped in front of a group of clothed people, or any variation on that theme, is a very blurry combination of 'look at me' and 'I'm ashamed'. Even classic humiliating activities – such as being pissed on – have somehow got an air of exhibitionism about them too.

Pain, for me, is something a bit different. Pain can feel humiliating to me, but usually it's too . . . painful to concentrate on that. The first time I was caned was up there with taking psychedelics – an insane sensory overload. There's heat and light and so much adrenaline, but also this sense of playing with an edge. *Can I take any more? I can't, I can't – no I can . . . I am trusting this person with my body and my brain . . . Can I trust them?* And then there's this huge rush of love and gratitude for them afterwards. It's beautiful but rare for me to find those people. Caning, flogging, whipping: these are really hard physical skills to perfect. A tentative spank is like a bad, too-light massage, and if someone isn't inspiring confidence in their skills, it's impossible to relax into the trance-like, extremely present state required – you just worry they'll take your eye out.

As I met more people, I learned that kink isn't always sex, or even sexual – in fact, people can get highly offended by the notion that it is. For me, it is one hundred per cent arousal, but the people to whom I might want to surrender my skin might not be the same people I would like inside my cunt. As I began to play with others, perhaps the most beautiful thing of all, was hearing their stories and desires. There was such a rich tapestry of human feeling and creativity within people's kinks, and discovering that was just as much fun and just as interesting as learning more about my own body and mind. Every dom or sub is driven by a different set of neurons, their endocrine and nervous systems firing in their own unique way.

One of the most difficult things for me to reconcile, as I allowed my fantasies to become realities more often, was a sense that to be submissive was at best lazy, and at worst, extremely selfish. Like most women, the patriarchy has bequeathed me a definite sense that I should check everyone else is fine at all times, and that to give is better than to receive. Outside of the playroom, it feels like a moral duty to check glasses are full on social occasions, and that no one is left out or lonely. We feel the need to be responsible at work, and to ensure that things are in order at home. Of course, the dominant is getting off on the fact that you are surrendering all of that, but I came to realise that a submissive, or a *good* submissive, which I had initially thought of as being the very easy ride side of the equation, actually does have skills to be proud of. Apparently not so many people are able to get out of their anxious heads enough to be fully present and willingly vulnerable, and fewer still to breathe through ten cracks of a bullwhip across their back.

So after a while, I began to feel a strange pride in being able to offer something to people who wanted it – needed it – which might be hard to find. A pride, might I add, that invariably comes before an exquisitely painful and humiliating fall, should I ever exhibit it.

Depictions of BDSM in popular culture are at best exasperating, and at worst prejudiced and offensive. Subs and doms are *always* presented as having a history of mental illness: see Christian Grey's childhood trauma, or Lee Holloway's suicide attempt and self-harming in *Secretary*. Even in the amazing *Nymphomaniac*, I don't think we see Charlotte Gainsbourg's character Joe as very . . . mentally well. Dominant women always dress like Catwoman, and BDSM men are usually genuine serial-killing psychopaths à la *American Psycho* or *Seven*. In Hollywood, if you are into kink of any kind, this is your whole identity. For me, it's not even my whole sexual identity – I like a slow, languid, skin-on-skin spooning on a Sunday morning, or a vanilla foursome on the sofa after a nice Ottolenghi dinner party, as much as the next person. To paraphrase Christopher Nolan's Batman, 'It's not who I am, it's something I sometimes like to do.' And guess what? The rest of the time, I like going to the pub, watching Netflix, working out, cooking roast dinners, and playing with my nieces and nephews on the beach. Some friends know about my occasional adventures, some don't (my religious mother certainly does not). I'm not ashamed of them, apart from in a hot way, but I know that for some people, it would become my entire self for them. Also, it's a bit . . . braggy. 'Kink bores' are up there with 'drug bores', and we've all heard the adage about how sex is like money – if you have lots of it, you don't talk about it.

My inclination and ability to schedule kinky fun ebbs and flows, largely due to other parts of life taking up more time. A busy phase at work, a family illness or a friend in crisis can make it unappealing or impossible for weeks or months. But I've noticed that during periods when I am able to skip off for hours of happy deviance on the regular, I feel calmer, happier, empowered and more positive about life. It's partly because having a bunch of orgasms caused by other people tends to do that, but I think there is something more. I think that the state you have to go to when submitting is extremely mindful – there is no way you cannot be present, because there's just too much going on with your body for you to get distracted by tomorrow morning's meeting or the fact you need to get the dishwasher fixed. More than that, I think if you can learn to be calm and accepting in the face of pain and humiliation in the safe – albeit testing – microcosm of a submissive session, your subconscious remembers this, and when you encounter stress in day-to-day life, these skills kick in automatically. After all, you have practised them. Yoga teaches the same thing, but with fewer ball gags.

As I tried more things and met more people, I realised that I wanted to record my experiences. Writing things down helped me think them through, particularly at first when I was trying to understand complicated issues around consent within a BDSM context, for example, and how to articulate my own desires and listen to those of others. I also realised that with every experience I chronicled in my journal, I was developing an excellent reserve of home-made, completely personalised, porn.

Max loved reading my diary, sometimes telling me to write it as he watched, seeing me get turned on as I recounted in type how I had been humiliated, beaten, fucked. Sometimes he made me read it to him, loving watching me get shy and embarrassed as I described aloud how slutty and perverted I had been. I began to share extracts with the people they involved, as a literary memento of a fun night. Dominants seemed to find it fascinating to learn what I had been thinking during a session. It often led to them revealing what had been going through their own minds; in fact, one of them wrote his version of the same session, and it was very illuminating.

I began to see my diary as a celebration – of being curious about people and the vastly beautiful range of physical and emotional feelings we can inspire in each other. From a union of minds, thinking and talking and finding out we're not alone in our weird desires, to accessing bodily sensations we have never dreamed of, playing with other people can be scary, comforting, painful, soulful, adrenaline-spiking, tear-inducing, euphoric, multi-orgasmic . . . and often, pretty funny. To me, that feels sublime.

I wonder if you might like reading it too. You might be shocked; you might be intrigued, turned on, aghast. You might want to call some doctors. All I ask is that you come to it with an open mind. Leave your expectations at the door. Submit.

Mind

How does a thought become action?

As Max and I decided to learn more about kink, and to see if our fantasies could work in the real world, we were wide-eyed, excited, enthusiastic, curious and completely ignorant. A fantasy in your mind is entirely under your control; you are an omniscient puppet-master. It stops and starts when you feel like it, or at least when it really is time to go to work. When you begin to play with other people, there is a major unknown in the equation – *them*. The idea of 'acting out your fantasies' turned out to be a misnomer. You cannot act them out, you can communicate them to others and see if together you can use them as inspiration to create a new, unique experience between you. If I have a fantasy of, say, being tied to a bed, blindfolded and teased, in my fantasy all the details work because they just *do*. But in reality, what am I tied up with? Do silk scarves feel nice or pathetic? Do handcuffs feel serious or too painful? Are my legs spread or are they hog-tied? How hot is it? What can I smell? What is teasing me? Am I being stroked by a feather or menacingly caressed by the tip of a cane? Are my boobs being squeezed? Are the hands big or small, rough or smooth? How many hands are there? And most importantly of all, *how do I say when I want it to stop and be sure that it will?*

As we began to meet people who were into kink, we realised we had so much to learn. There were so many strange words and acronyms, sometimes bizarre-seeming etiquette, and safety-conscious good practice. Our bookshelves filled up with the practical (*Shibari for Beginners*, *BDSM Basics*), the psychological (*Playing Well With Others*, *The Ethical Slut*), and the inspirational (literally everything from the Marquis de Sade to *The Way of a Man with a Maid* to Anaïs Nin). We went to workshops. We thought a lot and talked a lot. We made mistakes and went to some absolutely awful events. We met some lifelong friends, and some singularly odd people.

When you do not share a fantasy or kink, it seems impossible to believe, disgusting, repellent or maybe morally wrong. This is where prejudice comes from. If you cannot imagine being aroused by pain, it is so easy to assume that anyone who is must be damaged in some way. It doesn't help that psychology has pathologised all 'abnormal' desire from Freud onwards. It was only in 1973 that the American Psychiatric Association removed homosexuality from the *DSM*, their compendium of mental disorders, and it still states that cross-dressing, sadism, masochism, exhibitionism and voyeurism, amongst many, many other common sexual desires, are 'paraphilic' disorders, which should be treated as sicknesses.

In his brilliant book *Tell Me What You Want: The Science of Sexual Desire and How It Can Help You Improve Your Sex Life*, social psychologist Dr Justin J. Lehmiller analyses the results of his major study of sexual fantasy in the US, the largest ever. Only four per cent of women and seven per cent of men have *never* had a BDSM fantasy. Sixty-three per cent of women have forced-sex fantasies. Eighty-seven per cent of women have group sex fantasies. Forty-five per cent of people fantasise about fetish objects, and forty-two per cent about exhibitionism.

I learned that most of my desires can be described as BDSM (bondage, discipline, dominance, submission, sadism, masochism), multiplayer (group sex), and exhibitionist (being knowingly watched). I liked playing with men, women and the non-binary equally. I learned that I had little interest in voyeurism (watching people unbeknownst to them) or fetish (particular objects or body parts). I loved the idea of piss, hated the idea of shit.

It was easy to have a knee-jerk reaction if someone suggested something that would never work for me – *that's disgusting, how dare they suggest that!* But one of the loveliest lessons we learned was tolerance and acceptance. You might not want to piss on me, and I might not want to dress up as an animal, but that doesn't mean we cannot respect each other's beautiful weirdness – which is usually not so very weird at all. And sometimes, things you might never have expected to like turn out to be your very favourites. How will you ever know unless you try?

Max and I loved to describe our fantasies during sex, spilling our secret desires to make each other even more excited, developing the plotlines together. Some of our favourites were variations on the theme of 'Sonnet gets fucked by multiple anonymous men'. I don't know who went there first, but Max could tell that when he pinned down my thighs, describing how he would hold me down for one guy after another to enter me, my cunt would clench and spasm around his cock, and when I replied by describing how they would all come on me at the same time, covering me all over, I could feel him get even harder inside me. The idea of being used like this, and of Max watching and getting off on it, was somehow the hottest idea ever for us both. I don't think it's a particularly unusual one, although I was certainly more comfortable describing this kind of fantasy aloud during sex with Max than I had been with other partners. He felt unshockable and, if anything, impressed, which made me braver.

How do we know which of our fantasies should stay in our minds, and which will be even better in reality? With a willing partner in crime – who had, through a combination of being mischievous and down to earth, swiftly made me feel like the world was a playground, full of fun – the cavernous gap between imagination and possible reality seemed to be closing. After a particularly energetic and elaborate co-fantasy session, Max said, 'You know, I could make this happen for you in real life. Would you like that?'

I said I would love it, but wouldn't the logistics be insurmountable?

'Leave that to me,' he said.

One bright Tuesday morning in May, Max told me to meet him that evening at the Cross Keys pub in Covent Garden, and to wear a short dress and heels. As this is not the kind of outfit you would normally wear to a classic old-man pub, I suspected he had some kind of devious plan afoot. I spent the day at work distracted, excited and nervous. I got changed in the loos into an electric blue Agent Provocateur bra and knickers, a little black dress, and black heels, the highest I could actually walk in.

My boss came out of the next cubicle. 'Oh, you're all dressed up! Where are you off to?'

'Er . . . birthday party?' I mumbled, hoping she couldn't see me blush, while simultaneously feeling that sharp thrill of having a secret life. I am terrible at keeping my own secrets, and usually overshare everything, including in the office, but I was enjoying our burgeoning private kink life being something no one suspected. In this instance, though, I couldn't have told her what was about to happen even if I had wanted to.

I got to the pub at 7 p.m. Max texted and told me to wait there and order a drink. I got a gin and tonic and found a seat at the back, feeling self-consciously overdressed and increasingly nervous. Max came in after about twenty minutes. He had an air of general depravity about him, I could tell he was proud of whatever he was doing.

'You're such a menace!' I said.

He smiled back as if to say, *You have no idea*.

He took me out of the pub and led me down the street while I tried to guess what we were doing. He just kept smiling and saying, 'You'll see'.

We crossed the road and went into a Travelodge; I was giggling nervously about the seediness and joking, 'Oh it's a romantic mini-break – you shouldn't have!'

He took me up in the lift and down a corridor. We stopped in front of a room door.

'Take off your dress,' he commanded.

I seemed to be constantly naked in public since getting to know Max. I pulled my dress over my head and handed it to him. He kissed me, and pushed his hand inside my knickers and into my already pretty overexcited cunt. He pulled it out and sucked his fingers, smiling. Then he produced a scarf from his pocket and tied it around my eyes, checking I definitely couldn't see through it. I stood nearly naked and blindfolded in the Travelodge corridor for what felt like an eternity.

Then I heard the click of the door, and Max guided me through into the room. I could hear breathing, and I could tell there were people there, but not how many.

'Kneel,' Max said.

Wobbling slightly, I dropped to my knees.

'Open your mouth.'

I did, and I felt a hand around my head, and a cock thrust deep into my open mouth. I knew it did not belong to Max. I sensed other people around me, and felt eyes on me, as I sucked the anonymous man's cock. He pulled out, and before I could get my breath, another cock filled my throat. It was bigger and I choked. I heard a chuckle from above me. 'Take it!' the voice said, and a hand slapped my face. I tilted back my head and opened my throat as wide as I could. He fucked it relentlessly, and I felt my eyes water and tears run down my cheeks under the blindfold. He pulled out, and was replaced immediately by another. This man told me to suck his balls, and as I did, I felt hands on me, pulling my tits out of my bra and tugging my nipples, making me gasp. I still wasn't sure how many men were in the room. They moved around me.

As they took turns to fuck my mouth, I began to recognise the different cocks, the size and shape, the smoothness, the hardness, the taste – a drop of cum, the tiniest tang of urine, sweat. Having my sight removed made me focus on these feelings in my mouth – it was an enforced form of mindfulness, like the famous exercise where you let a square of chocolate melt on your tongue very slowly, and find you can taste so much more than usual. My brain wanted to identify and classify, as we always do when we meet new people, and it was so novel to have only their cocks, and occasionally their voices, to place them. Our senses, apparently, are not distinct in our brains. So we might think we are tasting something, but we're actually taking a visual cue. Shampoo manufacturers have found that apple-scented shampoo makes hair feel shinier to touch. Food that looks nicer also tastes better. Most of us don't spend a lot of time focusing on where our sensory inputs are coming from. Now, blindfolded and on my knees, I was on high alert, and so much more aware of the minutiae of variety, the different skin textures, the different feelings of their breath on me from above.

Eventually, I heard Max say, 'I think she should see what she is doing now,' and the blindfold was pulled from my face. I looked around.

There were five naked men standing in a circle around me, four watching, holding their erect cocks, all wet and glistening from my mouth, while the fifth's was in my hand. Max stood at the side, topless but still in jeans, holding one of his prized vintage cameras. I reflected it was a good thing he knew how to develop his own pictures. The men were a racially diverse group, of differing heights and builds, but all extremely muscular and confident, sure of their bodies and of their sexual performance, and clearly happy to be photographed in a gang bang. I wondered where Max had managed to find them.

I didn't have much time to look around. The guy currently in front of me looked over at Max enquiringly. Max nodded. The man looked back down at me and smiled. 'On all fours.'

I put my hands down and arched my back.

'Show them your cunt,' said Max.

I dropped my chest and chin to the ground and lifted my hands to pull my arse cheeks apart so they could all see better.

'Oh, what a pretty little cunt.'

'Look how wet she is, the little slut.'

'It wants to be fucked so hard.'

They all looked at me and made comments. I felt fingers thrust into me and gasped out, realising I was close to coming.

They laughed.

'She wants it so bad – shall we put her out of her misery?'

I heard the tear of condom wrappers, and suddenly my arse was pulled back as I felt the first cock enter me. I pushed up onto my hands so I could lean back into him, and looked round. It was the tanned Californian-looking blond. He frowned at me and slapped my arse. 'Look forwards.'

I did, and saw the shorter guy with weightlifting arms had appeared in front of me. I reached up for his cock and put it into my mouth. He thrust into me from the front as the other man fucked me from behind, all the others watching and wanking over the scene in front of them.

They moved me onto the bed, and the men rotated. The tallest man, who had lithe, climber limbs, knelt over me and put my ankles on his shoulders, folding me in half. His cock hit the back of my cunt and I cried out; this made him thrust deeper. In the meantime, two others knelt over my face, and alternated pushing their cocks into my mouth as I licked and sucked them furiously. I was coming again and again; the sensory overload seemed to have acted as a release valve deep inside. I lost track of who was where and who was fucking me. They flung me around the bed, getting greedier. At some point, Max lost the jeans and the camera and was there too, his hands pushing me down and holding me still for the others.

'I think it's time,' he said eventually.

They all pulled back and knelt around me on the bed, with me on my back. Someone took my hand and placed it on my cunt, which was raw and sore, vibrating and throbbing. They all looked down at me and began to rub their cocks furiously. I knew what was going to happen. I rubbed my clit and couldn't stop myself from coming even more. As I cried out, the first stream of cum hit my face, followed by five more all over my body.

Everyone panted, getting their breath back, muttering, 'Fuck me.' I felt cum roll across my belly and down my inner thighs.

I sat up, feeling almost stoned. We all started giggling.

'Well, that's not your average Tuesday night'.

Everyone started moving around, sitting on the bed or the chairs, and we had some surreal small talk. I wiped the cum from my eyes as I asked if this was a regular occurrence for them, or a first-time thing. Is there a gang-bang circuit out there you can get on? They all seemed to be nice, ordinary London guys. Max began to usher them out – I think he didn't want my chatter to ruin the anonymity, maybe.

When they had gone, he stretched out on the bed next to me and brushed the sweaty, sticky hair from my face. 'I fucking love you, you total deviant slut.'

My second-ever date with Max was at Gordon's Wine Bar, an ancient, dark, cave-like space near Charing Cross, where condensation drips down as you huddle into tables separated by iron railings. Our first date a week earlier had involved a crawl round Soho's diviest bars, getting increasingly drunk and increasingly tactile, until I had made the inspired suggestion of using my twenty-four-hour pass to sneak us into my office building, where we consummated our five-hour relationship on the large, shiny oak table in the boardroom, something I had long been fantasising about during interminable company meetings. I had spent the week itching to see Max again, scanning the office for CCTV cameras, and wondering if Bruce, the kindly old security guard, was smirking at me every morning.

It was a wet, cold December Thursday. We crouched into one of the dark corners with a carafe of sticky blackberry-scented *vin de table*. Soon we were having one of those second-date get-to-know you chats, only we had somehow skipped over how many brothers and sisters we each had, and got quickly onto more interesting details.

Max told me he had been volunteering himself online for threesomes – usually with a heterosexual couple who wanted an extra pair of hands. My mind was blown; all the straight men I had known were all for two women attending to them, but were somehow afraid of sharing me with another man. Max, conversely, described how hot this was for him – he loved the idea of a woman so up for cock she wanted two of them at the same time. He thought it was beautiful and empowered. For him, 'slutty' could only be a term of pride.

I told him about the sex parties I had been to, and their pros and cons. He said he would love to go to one. He told me he had been to a fetish night. He had been more of a spectator, but he had seen people flogged and restrained, slaves at the mercy of masters. 'It was hot.'

He said that so nonchalantly that somehow, for the first time ever, it felt completely OK to say that this might be something I was into. He might even be impressed! I told him about my dog-eared copy of *The Story of O* – and recounted the plot for him. A beautiful young woman called O – her name, just a hole – is taken by her lover to a chateau in Roissy which is home to a special society of men. There, she is trained to be a submissive sex slave. She is constantly chained, whipped, stripped, beaten and fucked in the mouth, cunt or arse whenever the men want. Her arsehole is stretched by butt plugs. Her labia is pierced and an identifying metal tag is hung from it, and a leash from that. In the grand tradition of French erotica, it won a prestigious literary prize and was also banned. Misguided feminists in the sixties decreed that it must have been written by a man – the author was anonymous – but I knew no man could have described a woman's submissive fantasy in such glorious physical detail.

I told Max I read it often before bed, imagining myself into O's shoes, but had never even really thought about seeking out those kinds of experiences in real life, or even whether it was possible to do so. By this time, we were close on the banquette, and his hand was slipping under my skirt, while I was stroking the growing bulge in his trousers.

'Well,' said Max. 'Maybe we should try and find out. I'll do some research.'

That night, we couldn't wait to get home to one of our flats, and he ended up fucking me in the arse in a damp alcove on a back street – in, as we discovered halfway through, full view of a rough sleeper.

It seemed like an auspicious start.

❧

As we got to know each other better over the coming months, our relationship developed on two parallel train tracks. On one, we discovered each other's taste in music and film, in books and pizza toppings. We huddled under the duvet in each other's flatshares, as the spring refused to come, too skint to pay for heating. We chain-smoked and drank cheap wine, talked about our career ambitions and whether we could get Glastonbury tickets. On the other, we began to learn about the kink universe, which, it seemed, was all around us. We signed up to nude photography and fetish websites; in this pre-app time, they were kinky versions of Myspace or Facebook. We waited till my housemates were out and self-styled a kink photoshoot, trying to use cunning lighting to make ourselves look both sexy and unidentifiable. We made joint profiles and explained we were new to the scene and looking to try . . . pretty much anything. We immediately got messages – I felt like we were fresh meat to the community, and I loved that feeling. Max took on the role of screening and replying and planning dates. We set up a special joint Google calendar, and joked about how happy our bosses would be if either of us exhibited these levels of organisation at work.

We would go for a drink with a man or woman, couple or throuple, and our eyes would widen as they regaled us with tales of their adventures. We learned that people *love* to give advice and show off about the crazy things they get up to, and we were very, very willing new recruits. I often felt shy and inarticulate, and had to ask what something meant every couple of minutes. But people told us about workshops we could attend, books we could read. We went to a rope bondage day, where Max learned to tie beautiful shibari knots around me, and it put me into a strange, aroused trance. We made dents in our overdrafts buying toys our new friends recommended and learned how to use them: restraints, butt plugs, paddles. The 'incognito' windows on our browsers got a lot of use, as we tried to avoid sharing our new interests with our employers.

Max kept suggesting we go to a 'Munch'. I was resistant. The name alone was extremely off-putting – it hardly conjured the heights of heady sexual adventure we were seeking. A Munch, apparently, was a purely social event held by a kink group where people could meet each other just to talk, outside of the dungeon or the night itself. To me, this sounded horrific. I liked chatting to people on a date, but a big group? Isn't that a bit like a WI meeting? Max was cajoling: 'You'll meet nice people. Or weird, strange people. They will tell you about things you've never even thought of. They will invite you to places we've never heard of. It's a couple of hours on a Saturday – come on!'

I grumpily capitulated. I was quite judgemental when I saw that the venue was a particularly awful tourist pub. I was even more judgemental when we climbed the stairs to the private room, and all I could see was 'amusing' hats, blue hair and tartan-print Doc Martens. I hated the stereotypical idea that to be into anything 'alternative' sexually, you had to look 'alternative', and that your whole identity and aesthetic was determined by whatever your predilections in the bedroom happened to be. It reminded me of my friend Steph railing against the fact everyone always assumed she was vegan because she happened to exclusively fuck women. 'I eat cunt. I still eat steak,' she would growl, when presented with an earth-mother beansprout salad.

A man with a sequined stovepipe hat came over to us. He beamed welcomingly. 'You must be Max and Sonnet? So lovely to meet you. Welcome to our Munch.'

Max looked at me as if to say, *See? Here is a nice, friendly man.*

I thawed a bit; after all, it is nice to be greeted when you walk in feeling a bit lost and encounter a big group of people who seem to know each other, even if they had stupid hats on.

He introduced himself. Then he asked us, 'If you were animals, what animals would you be?'

I had a strong memory of a group interview I'd attended at my local high street branch of Gap at the age of fifteen. They'd asked us which vegetable we identified with. *So zany! You don't have to be mad to work here, but . . .*

Max managed to grip my hand before I said anything sarcastic.

The Ringmaster took us over to a group of people who were chatting, and introduced us as 'Kestrel' and 'Ferret', identifications which had more to do with both of us having just finished *H Is for Hawk* than deep personality traits.

We spent the next hour meeting people and listening to their stories. One girl told us how she had felt lonely in London, having moved here from abroad, and had found the community to be a lifeline. A guy told us how this group was the first place he had been able to open up about his bisexuality. It was about so much more than the 'play', we kept hearing. It was fascinating, and sad, to hear how, for some people, the loneliness or shame they felt about their kinks had leaked into the rest of their lives, leaving them feeling uncomfortable and unaccepted in other communities. Finally, they had found a group of people in London with whom they could be themselves – for some of them, on a daily basis, whether for coffee, the cinema or summer picnics. It was completely different to how Max and I felt. For us, this world was absolutely separate, and at this point completely hidden, from our daily lives and friends. But, as we said to each other later, it was pure luck and privilege that the urges we had felt, while occasionally making us feel secretly ashamed or 'weird', had not led us to distance ourselves from people we perceived as 'normal'.

A smiley woman with pink hair, blue lipstick and absolutely gigantic tits explained how she always felt like she was 'passing'; she hated to feel like she was pretending to be someone she wasn't when with other communities or friendship groups. I was so interested in that viewpoint. If I'm at a godchild's birthday party, playing *Twister* with the kids or chatting to the parents about the latest HBO drama, I don't feel like I am masquerading – I feel like myself then too. I am just as much 'me' then, as I am when spreadeagled over a pommel horse with a butt plug in my arse.

We got talking to a male/female couple named Neil and Sarah. They asked if we fancied going outside for a cigarette. We acquiesced for a bit of a break – and because, as we communicated to each other with our eyes, we both thought they were hot.

Outside, Neil smiled roguishly. 'You're swingers too, aren't you? I can tell.'

'I mean . . . yes, but what do you mean?' I was puzzled.

'We're the outcasts from the group! They just about tolerate us, but we'll never make the inner circle with our slutty, sex-greedy ways.'

'OK, I am so confused. I thought this whole group was about accepting people's unconventional sexual urges?'

'Ah, no . . . this group is about fetish and BDSM. Swapping partners, group sex, that doesn't count. BDSM is not the same as sex. Lots of the people up there – they would never have sex with anyone outside of a monogamous relationship, and their kinks don't involve nudity or "vanilla" sexual practices – they *only* involve spanking or needle play or roleplay or whatever.'

'Yeah,' said Sarah. 'One time, this guy – I think you met him? The one with the big dermal piercings at the base of his throat? He was giving my nipples these little electric shocks with some fun gadget, as I lay backwards over a box, and as he walked round me, I saw the bulge in his leather shorts, so I invited him to fuck my mouth. Turns out, that was a *total* faux pas.'

It is truly amazing how humans manage to codify and invent rules and manners for any kind of community or situation. For those inside the community who feel like they belong, they do not even think of these as rules, as such; they have become instinctive. For those looking in, these conventions can feel cliquey and exclusive. I felt in part repulsed by the notion of there being a specific code of behaviour or manners for a sex and kink community, but in part excited to learn them and be inculcated into it.

'God, I would never have thought of that! What a minefield. It's not like you grabbed his cock without consent, you just asked!'

'I think it immediately identified us with the rival, *swinging* community, which they seem to look down on a bit,' said Neil.

'So what about us made you think "wife-swapping" rather than "kink only"?' asked Max.

'Oh, purely wishful thinking,' said Neil, touching my arm.

'Interesting,' said Max, reaching up to stroke Sarah's long, silky hair. 'I think we are pretty wishful too . . .'

Over those early months, Max and I went to parties, to clubs, to the furthest reaches of the internet. We were each emboldened by having the other as a partner in crime. He loved seeing me enjoy new things, and how game I was to give them a try. I loved how *competent* he was. He could pick up skills so easily. Quickly, people started lining up to be spanked by him, and I could have sworn he was growing special muscles in his right arm as a result. We loved giggling and texting during the week about what strange situations we had found ourselves in at the weekend. I could see how much he loved seeing me with others, or stripping naked in front of a group. To me, this felt so searingly generous, and I fell a little bit more in love with him every time. I loved how he would gently push me, encouraging me to offer my arse to a guy with a flogger or my tits to a girl with some dripping hot wax.

We would get home late, too wired to sleep, fucking again and again as we recounted all the things we had seen and done.

We wanted to push the boundaries ever further, into different realms and worlds full of difference people. And we did meet people, from across the whole stretch of human experience.

We were approached by The Contessa on a fetish website. She invited us to an extremely exclusive, highly selective party. *We've arrived!* we thought. *We're in a special club! We must be the Kink Elite.*

It was a masquerade, with implications of untold debauchery. I imagined 'The Masque of the Red Death', rooms of exquisite luxury making way for dungeons of untold darkness. I pictured both silk brocade chaises longues, and well-used relics dating from the time of the Spanish Inquisition.

The address was in Mayfair, an intimidatingly grand postcode. We arrived damp, having walked from the Tube, feeling inadequate for not having a Bentley. The venue was indeed on a posh street, but the door was unprepossessing. There was no Georgian staircase, and it looked more like it had been added to the building later as a staff entrance. The paint was peeling.

'Is this the right number?' I asked Max.

He shrugged. 'Seems to be?'

We pressed the wonky plastic doorbell – there was no shining brass knocker or thick red rope bell pull, or indeed, a butler. We heard footsteps shuffling down a clearly uncarpeted staircase.

A man opened the door. He had thinning hair and a paunch. 'Come in, come in,' he said. 'Up there.' He gestured to a staircase.

We went up to a first-floor flat. It looked like a safe house from a John le Carré novel, sparsely furnished with offcuts from other, more loved apartments.

'Would you like a drink? Let me take your coats.' We reluctantly handed them over.

He returned with two thin plastic disposable cups, filled with a sweet, sticky cava. Then he shuffled off.

We seemed to be half the age of everyone else. There were a few women, but mostly there were men, who en masse bore a striking resemblance to the Tory backbench.

'Oh my god, what shall we do?' I muttered to Max, while fixing a polite grin to my face.

'Let's go into the hall,' he replied, sotto voce. We edged out gingerly, as if George Smiley was about to reveal us as Russian spies.

In the hallway, we debated whether we should leave, if that would be incredibly rude, and where our coats were. Maybe we should just abandon them. This party was clearly so different to what we'd been expecting. We felt stupid and like we had been conned. It was as if all the stereotypes about the kink and swinging world were true – they were populated by entitled rich people, and everyone looked a bit gross and possibly a bit shady.

At that moment, two other people appeared on the stairwell, a man and a woman about our own age. They had a similar air of shiftiness, and were speaking in stage whispers.

'No, I want to leave, *right now*,' hissed the woman.

'Oh, sorry, hello . . .' the man said, on seeing us.

We all smiled awkwardly.

'So . . . what the hell *is* this party?' said the man.

'I know, right?' I said. 'I just don't think I'll . . . have the right small talk.'

'What, you can't talk about the time you sighted the Big Five on safari in Kenya?' said the woman.

'More like, shot the Big Five in Rhodesia,' muttered Max.

We laughed and introduced ourselves. They were called Robin and Sally, and had got the Tube up from Balham.

'What are the Big Five, anyway?' said Robin.

'One must definitely be a lion.'

'Yes, and an elephant.'

'Rhino?'

'Leopard, maybe?'

'Tiger?' said Robin.

'What, in Africa?' said Sally. 'I think you only get to hunt them when you're posted to the Raj . . .'

'Since when are you an expert on colonial history?'

Buoyed up with the bravado of new comrades in arms, we decided to mount Operation Coat-check.

There was a staircase up to another floor. It looked promising.

We climbed the stairs and tried the first door. It was a small, dingy bedroom, in which a large bed had been placed awkwardly, so you couldn't quite walk around it. The bed was covered in a shiny black sheet.

'Riiight.'

Suddenly, we heard footsteps outside. Robin swiftly closed the door and put his back to it.

'Shhhhhh,' he said. 'We better stay in here until the coast is clear. Oh wait, there's a lock. That is weird. But handy.'

He clicked the lock. We all looked at each other, and sat down on the shiny bed. The good thing about sex parties, I thought, is that even when they are terrible, you know why you are there, and it is simply a lot easier to thus initiate sex than it is in 'normal' life. You are in a room, with a bed, and probably a bowl of condoms and a couple of lube dispensers. And while they might not necessarily want to fuck *you*, the people there are definitely DTF in general.

The high drama of our Cold War espionage escape plans made way for an enjoyable foursome. At one point, when Robin's cock was in my mouth, and I felt mounting excitement, assuming he was about to come down my throat . . .

He suddenly shouted: 'BUFFALO! That's the fifth animal! It's definitely a buffalo!'

We stayed friends with Robin and Sally for many years, often shouting out big-game animals whenever anyone was about to come. The party had taught us some wise lessons. Firstly, it is unlikely there is a secret 'kink elite' to which you can be invited. There are all sorts of people, having all sorts of parties, and some are good and some are bad – and your bad might be someone else's good. Secondly, even if they are awful, what's the worst that can happen? Some social awkwardness, and then you leave. Far from discouraging us, the shittest parties tended to make us more confident – if we could survive, unscathed, a room of creepy old right-wing politicians, what couldn't we weather? And thirdly – and this is an excellent moral for life – even in the darkest of times, you can meet a really funny, sexy couple.

There is a bitchy stereotype that kink is 'how ugly people get laid'. This is nonsense; what you look like has very little to do with what your sexual peccadillos might be, and the ratio of conventionally beautiful people who are into kink seems exactly the same as in normal life.

But as we met more self-proclaimed kink people, I realised my ideas about attraction were changing. I was finding that energy, imagination, flair, competence, and complementary desires, was far more important than looks. If Ryan Gosling has never flogged anyone before, I don't think I want him to try it out on me.

Whereas traditional dating culture has become more and more reduced to looks thanks to our swipe-right app-based universe, in kink dating people are much more interested in what you want to do than how you look.

I found that I was often attracted to older doms, because they immediately gave off an air of experience. A twenty-year age gap might have felt strange to me if we were dating, but if they were going to be using complex bondage restraints, their age added to my sense of trust.

My preconceptions kept being challenged. I assumed I would find it hard to be dominated by a man physically smaller than me – it was such an imbedded cultural belief that in men, size equals power. But then I met Andrew. He and his partner Jenny were great fun. They had turned a tiny new-build apartment in south London into a brilliant dungeon. I was always asking where they put everything when their parents came round. We had originally connected with them on a fetish site, but were always bumping into them at events, and they sometimes had small parties at their flat. Andrew was short, and of a small build, but he had an intense focus and a particularly deviant, dangerous sort of energy. He was incredibly creative and loved trying new things.

He told me one day that he had been studying and practising erotic hypnosis. This is where you hypnotise someone, and then make sexual suggestions for them to carry out. I immediately loved the idea of being completely at someone's mercy in this way; it was like bondage, but mental. I had long suspected I would be an excellent candidate for hypnosis because I am completely suggestible. If someone describes a cake they ate, I feel like I can taste it . . . and really want to eat it myself. If I read a book set in the Arctic, I get physically cold. I am an advertiser's dream. You're right, I *do* want to drive that car on the open road! I can *feel* how refreshing that Coke is! Oooohhhh, warming lube? My cunt is now wet. (How did you know, Instagram? Are you listening?)

I told Andrew I would love to try it. Max and I went round to theirs on a Saturday night with plans to try it out, alongside various other play. Andrew suggested we start with the hypnosis, as he thought it would put me in an excellent headspace for the rest of the evening. I concurred. He told me to sit in the comfy armchair, lean back and relax. Max and Jenny got drinks and settled themselves on the sofa opposite to watch, knowing the sense of exhibitionism would be good for me, but also out of curiosity.

I was to stay fully clothed, which surprised me. Andrew pulled up a dining chair and sat opposite me. He told me to close my eyes, and began to talk me through a breathing exercise. It was reminiscent of guided meditation, and I could feel the tension of the week melting away. His voice was authoritative but calm and slow, and I had no sense of how much time was passing. He told me to imagine myself naked on a beach, the sand melting into my skin. I felt warm all over. And I realised that I *felt* naked, even though I knew I wasn't; I couldn't feel my clothes.

After a while, the voice, which I had stopped thinking of as being Andrew specifically, said it was going to give me some instructions.

'First of all, lift up your right arm.'

I thought this was a boring instruction, and that of course I didn't *have* to lift my arm up, but why not? I lifted it up.

'Great. You are under my control.' His tone changed slightly.

I felt immediately that I was in a place of surrender, but I also really felt extremely relaxed and warm and comfortable. It was a different sort of feeling to the more adrenaline-fuelled excitement I usually feel as a submissive.

'Your cunt is going to be the wettest it has ever been. Lie back and feel it begin to gush. You're not going to be able to help it. Relax, and let it happen.'

Again, I felt like if I didn't want to do this, I wouldn't. But I really did want to. So I lay back in the chair and had a vision of all the liquid in my body rushing like a waterfall to my cunt. Down from my head, up from my toes. I felt hot, and I could feel my cunt pulsing and my breath quickening.

'Good. Now I want you to open your eyes slowly, and look at me.'

I did as he said. He was calm and serious, and looking directly into my eyes.

'Good. Now I want you to undress slowly, fold your clothes and put them on this stool.'

I stood up slowly. I felt very liquid, like you do after a sauna and steam. I quietly took all my clothes off, folded them and deliberately placed them on the stool, then sat back down. Andrew was very still and silent as I did this. I had completely forgotten about Max and Jenny watching.

'Lie back and spread your legs. But do not close your eyes. Look at me. You want to show me how very, very wet you are.'

Somehow, that comment sent a pulse through my whole body, like an electromagnetic surge. I looked into his eyes and I had the feeling I was going to gush, even though no one had touched me.

'It is unbearable. It is a torrent. It feels like your very organs are being pulled out of your cunt. You can't stop it. You want to show me.'

I was aware that I was groaning as all of this became true.

'You know that the one thing you need to have the most intense orgasm of your life, is my cock pushed deep, deep into your throat. Lie backwards over the arm of the chair, and offer your mouth to me.'

I did so. He stood up, and slowly moved round the armchair, never losing my gaze. He took out his cock and pushed it straight into my mouth and down my throat.

'Your mouth and jaw are relaxed. They are elastic. You can be here for ever. This is where you are happiest. This is where you need to be. Showing me your gushing cunt, and wanting my cock so much. This is going to make you come so hard. You want to show me.'

I didn't want any of this to stop, but his voice and the images and the sense of his cock in my throat were causing a new wave through my body. I felt a flood pour out of my cunt. It wouldn't stop. He was thrusting into my mouth, and this was just making me come and come.

Finally, he pulled out, and walked back to his chair.

His voice went back to a soothing therapist tone.

I can't remember what he said, but I was aware of my breath returning to normal and feeling calm and relaxed.

'And now you're awake.'

I blinked open my eyes and looked around the room.

I saw Max and Jenny. Max was shaking his head and chuckling. Jenny said, 'I have never seen someone come like that without being touched at all'.

Andrew grinned. 'You're a great subject,' he said, and high-fived me.

I really don't know if I was genuinely hypnotised, or if I was going along with everything in a submissively obedient way, and it was just because the scenario itself was so arousing in itself. Maybe Paul McKenna's subjects also think, *Well, I don't necessarily have to do this, but I might as well*, and that's just how hypnotism works – I am not sure. I wonder if it was simply that being so incredibly relaxed was deeply powerful.

For the rest of the evening, I was hyper-aroused at everything, and generally in the best mood ever.

We tried erotic hypnosis another time, on the dancefloor at a fetish club night. Andrew was wondering if you could get the same effect in such a busy place of sensory overload. We stood still and I looked at him as he spoke and calmed me. Eventually, he told me to strip completely naked on the dancefloor and then touch myself in front of everyone. Again, I have no idea if I did this because I was hypnotically compelled to, or because he told me to as a dom.

After some of the most intense and weird orgasms of my life, I had a major rethink about shorter men as dominants, and thinking about Andrew makes me far more wet than any tall, broad Hollywood celeb.

A year into our relationship, Max and I had found ourselves in some surreal situations. We were like people joining a new gym and trying out all the classes to see if, in fact, 'Bambu Bodies' is the one for them. But we had always played together – one of us might be across the room with two different cocks in her mouth and cunt, but the other was still at the same party, maybe tying shibari on a submissive model or watching needle play.

Max had to go away for work for two months. He was adamant that I should not suffer a cruel, celibate fate for such a long period, and that I should date and meet other men and women while he was gone. There was part of me that was a bit offended – surely, love means that you are jealous if your partner sleeps with someone else, not completely blasé. That is what our culture has told us, on repeat, since at least the nineteenth century. But Max seemed to think the reverse: that if you love someone, especially someone who really, really likes having sex, above all you would want them to be happy, not deprived. He trusted me to see sex as a beautiful, fun, even silly activity, which did not suddenly turn into a romantic, exclusive relationship with someone else. But was this just a convenient theory, entirely created so that he could philander in the way that women are told all men want to?

Did he basically just want to cheat on me, have his cake and eat it, and was dressing it up as a generous act to me? Well, in this instance, his trip wasn't going to provide much opportunity, as it largely involved making a documentary in a remote part of Alaska, but in general he pointed out that this was a patriarchal stereotype, a subscription to the idea that a woman wants to ensnare a man who is a free, independent spirit, while her only need is to procreate.

Thinking it all through, I was keen to unpick this legacy of love equals jealousy, but I wasn't really sure how it would work. What if I slept with another man and he wanted something more? What if I did prefer him to Max? I had cheated on partners in the past – and, indeed, been cheated on – and the fallout was indescribably horrific. Could even an authorised extracurricular liaison lead to this kind of hurt and chaos? I couldn't bear the idea of that happening to Max and me. But then, was the cause of the hurt actually the fact that you'd slept with another person – which we had done plenty of times with the other present – or was it entirely down to the deception and the breaking of a promise? If we submitted to the idea that we trusted each other, and that loving someone did not mean they had to make a promise of monogamy to you, would it be possible to simply be happy for them and their enjoyment of someone else? And was it really so different from other kinds of hanging out? If Max had dinner with a friend, it wouldn't throw me into a spiral of anxiety, paranoia or jealousy, so if instead of eating food with someone he was fucking them, was it really so very different?

Happily, today there is far more conversation about 'ethical non-monogamy', or 'consensual non-monogamy' (if you don't want to imply you're morally superior to monogamous people), but this was the noughties, before Instagram and Feeld and the explosion of sex-positive content. Most people we had met so far seemed to belong to the fetish scene (which needn't involve sex, let alone relationships), or they were swingers (couples who had sex with other people together), or they were poly. We had met fully poly people, with two or three romantic partners of equal importance in their lives, and they were happy, evolved and excellent at communication, but to me, it just seemed like an extreme admin headache. Quite frankly, remembering to tell one person you're out at a work event was hard enough, and imagine navigating Christmas – two sets of families is plenty. But what we were discussing wasn't that. We were talking about separating sex and kink from the other parts of our relationship – everything from sharing our hopes and fears to splitting the council tax – making sex simply a highly enjoyable activity we both loved, and finding other people who saw it that way too.

But still, while I liked the theory, I told Max I didn't think I was comfortable enough to do a *normal* date while he was gone.

He chuckled. 'Right, but you'd be totally comfortable with being flogged naked in front a whole fetish club?'

I shrugged; to me, it seemed a different thing.

A couple of weeks into Max's trip, Jordan texted me. I had first met Jordan years earlier at one of those sex parties that tries to be glamorous, equates 'sexy' with 'pretending to be rich' and seems to come from the same events planning company who do those James Bond-themed corporate Christmas parties. The man I was with at the time was a big fan of threesomes, always with me and another twenty-four-year-old woman – he would definitely have said 'girl' – and he liked these parties to facilitate that. He would not entertain the idea of an 'MMF' threesome for a second – I never got to the bottom of whether that was because he thought it was 'a bit gay', or because he was jealous of my attentions going to another man. The idea of my attentions going to a woman was clearly unthreatening – as Nancy Friday writes: 'A woman lies down with another woman and the world shrugs.' I think he did not for a second believe in my bisexuality, and thought that women perform as lesbians purely for men, which turned him on.

At this party, we had met and chatted to Jordan, who was good-looking, chilled, funny and had clearly been around this scene for some time. I had exchanged numbers with him, mostly just wanting to be friends. A few days later, he rang me and asked if I ever played separately from my partner and might want to hang out, or whether we would be up for a threesome with him. I very much omitted to mention the first suggestion when relaying this to my partner, and even the second caused a big fight. But Jordan and I had texted every now and again, and when I described him to Max, Max suggested we all meet up. We had gone round to Jordan's warehouse flat in Tottenham, which had all manner of conveniently placed metal girders in the ceiling. Max and Jordan had got along immediately, and I could barely walk for days afterwards, each wince making me wet in memory.

I told Jordan that Max was away, and it would be nice to see him – but just to catch up. We arranged to go for Turkish food. I told Max, and he implored me on a daily basis to reconsider my position and fuck Jordan. He kept reminding me how many times Jordan had made me come and how massive his cock was, and describing his talents with ropes and floggers.

'IT'S JUST DINNER!' I would text back.

When I arrived at the restaurant, Jordan was already there. He was leaning against the wall in a plain black T-shirt, and his muscly arms immediately made me think of him pinning me down . . . but actually, as he enveloped me in a hug, I realised how much I liked him as a friend too. He had a slight twinkle in his eye, perhaps, but seemed absolutely prepared for an evening of just chatting and laughing. I realised I was the one getting more tactile. We were on a tiny table, and each time our elbows or knees brushed, my cunt twitched, but I tried to ignore it. Jordan seemed to be completely chilled.

When dessert arrived, he said, 'So by the way, Max messaged me . . .'

I raised my eyebrows. 'Oh, really? What did he say?'

'Well, he said that I should feel extremely free to take you home with me, perform unspeakable acts of depravity upon your naked body, and that it would make him very happy if this happened.'

I nearly spat out my baklava, but there was something incredibly hot about Max almost giving my body away;

as if it was an act of submission to him, to be fucked by Jordan.

Jordan smiled cheekily. 'But it's entirely up to you, my friend.'

I knew my resolve had weakened. Somehow, Max's involvement in the proceedings from afar was allaying my fears. Despite how like a 'normal' date the evening had been, I suddenly could see what might happen if I viewed it as a kink event, rather than the potential beginning of an illicit affair that would destabilise everything Max and I had together. My perspective had subtly shifted. I had no idea, then, what beautiful and exciting adventures that shift would herald over the next decade.

We ordered another glass of wine, and I completely gave in to noticing the feeling of his skin as his arm brushed mine, and looking at his lips as he talked.

He stopped mid-sentence. 'You want to fuck me so badly, don't you?'

I smiled sheepishly.

'Well, you will have to invite me, properly. Believe me, I love telling you what to do, but in this instance, whatever your cunt wants right now – and I mean, I can tell it's completely wet just by your face – it's your choice, and there is absolutely no pressure from me. Or from Max! We can easily just go for a nightcap or call it a night, or whatever.'

He was momentarily serious, and I realised how kind he was being. He knew this was new for me, and despite the fact we had known each other for so long and had played together in different ways, he was aware that this particular scenario was strange for me. It was the first of many times that I would conclude that consensually non-monogamous and kinky people think so seriously about the ethics of their sex lives that they seem to have more clarity around consent and what that really means than people within the standard heteronormative dating world do.

It was most reassuring . . . and it made me fancy him even more.

I felt like Buffy inviting Angel over the threshold. 'Right, I officially invite you to . . . fuck my brains out, OK?'

'Got it.' He looked over his shoulder. 'Cheque, please!'

My flat was round the corner. We nearly made it there, but Jordan pinned me against the wall outside and kissed me, pushing his hand inside my jeans.

'Oh, you are so ready for my cock . . .'

We tumbled inside and straight into the bedroom, our clothes seeming to fall off immediately. As his limbs encompassed me, all that conscious *thinking* evaporated in a world of heat and sweat and energy.

As we lay getting our breath back afterwards, Jordan suggested I send Max a selfie. I realised it was late enough that he might just be waking up on the other side of the world.

Jordan angled the camera so the dribble of cum on my nipple and the red streaks across my breasts were visible, along with his naked torso and well-used cock.

I sent the picture. A couple of minutes later my phone bleeped.

'This makes me so happy.'

'Also, I'm hard now.'

Thinking about it all much later – and for many years afterwards – I wondered if the traditional ideas about monogamy are born from a scarcity mindset. There seems to be a notion that you only have a finite amount of lust available, and if you use it up on someone else, you'll have none left for your partner, who will feel jealous and lacking. The trope of the cheating spouse who is full of raging lust in their affair, but lacks any desire for their husband or wife at home, is one we see again and again on screen. But even if that were true, might it be the *guilt* making enjoying the sex at home difficult, not the impossibility of managing to enjoy fucking two different people in a week? (Or four in an afternoon?)

We found that the reverse was true: the more sex we had with other partners, the more we wanted it with each other. Seeing Max desired by others makes him seem even hotter to me – and it makes me proud. If I spend an evening with someone else, I return hornier than ever, with sexy stories to recount. I love coming home at 7 a.m. after a night elsewhere, finding Max still in bed, and climbing on top of him, my cunt still stretched out by someone else. Max loves the idea of me being slutty, whether at a deliberately planned kink date, or on receiving that late-night, 'I just met someone at a party, I might go to theirs, if that's OK?' message. There is an understanding that we come first; we would never cancel plans with each other for someone else. We usually ask, and we always, always tell. We both know that even an innocent omission could hurt the other if discovered later; we are convinced it is lying and deceit that cause people problems, and in no way the sex itself.

Besides, why would we want to keep anything a secret, when it's so much fun to tell?

I always tell other partners I have a boyfriend; it's common enough now for people to be in a couple but not monogamous, and I am pretty happy to explain how it works for us. And while I will probably tell Max how they came on my face or fucked my arse, I wouldn't tell him their secrets, hopes and fears, in the same way that I wouldn't tell him something told to me in confidence by any other close friend. I have become friends with some of Max's other regular partners, and he with mine, but some we don't introduce. I have one friend, Anthony, with whom I have been playing for eight years. He and Max talk online sometimes, but I think it would feel odd for them to meet in person, because the dynamic is so choreographed with him, very intense and one-on-one . . . as you will see. In contrast, Max has a lovely friend named Tove. He mostly plays with her on his own, but I love going to the pub with her and hanging out, we occasionally have threesomes with her, and she actually came on holiday with us one time. She is our normal friend as well as his kinky friend.

For me, this is an abundant way to live. The sense that there is an infinite amount of love and lust in the universe, that the more you find, the more there will be, and the more you give out, the more you get back – to me, this feels like the way humans are meant to be. I know that there are people who love living truly monogamously, and I would never want to deny that this way of life exists. It's a kink, like any other, and while it might feel odd to me, to others it is natural and beautiful and sexy. But what is frustrating is the way people tend to *default* to monogamy, which causes so much hurt and shame for so many.

What could be nicer than navigating the world open to the idea that you might meet someone exciting, whether you are dating other people or not? Of looking outwards at strangers and wondering about them, rather than closing yourself off to them? Every day offers the possibility of meeting someone you might want to touch, or who might want to tie you up and piss on your face. And it's amazing how often that turns out to be true . . .

A work meeting had overrun, and it was pouring down with rain, so I was racing back home on my bike, feeling that I really, really didn't want to keep Darla the dom waiting. I quickly dropped off my bike at home and changed into some dry but very mundane clothes, then raced out to the bar.

When I arrived, there was a beautiful girl sitting outside on the bench, smoking. I knew it was her. She had the longest, svelte legs in the skinniest jeans; she was an undercut-sporting, leather-wearing, uber-queen hipster. I was completely intimidated.

I shouted 'Darla?' in a high-pitched voice, and she languidly smiled and stood up, towering over me. She kissed me on the cheek and ushered me into the bar.

We got drinks and sat on the high stools as the bar began to fill up. After five minutes of general chat, I discovered she was a pretty well-known musician, hosted some depraved parties and had a very cute Dalmatian puppy – and she discovered I was a deeply uncool, book-reading cyclist. But quickly, we got down to business. Darla said that she was looking for a girl sub, and had not yet found a satisfactory one. Apparently she had found that bi girls frequently prefer to be dommed by men. I thought that was a bit sad, as if the patriarchy was butting in, even in our inclusive kink universe.

Even at this point, I could feel my cunt twitching. She talked more and more about what she was looking for in a sub. She wanted a girl whom she could take to parties as her toy. She would ask whoever she wanted to fuck them; she would offer up her toy to men and women in front of everyone else. If everyone was dressed, she would make her toy go naked. Her sub would only ever do what Darla told her. She talked about having a pet: a sub who would behave like an animal and be treated like her dog. She wanted to go to a nice bar with her sub, and make her sub take off her knickers and expose herself in public. She wanted her sub to be publicly humiliated, and to be uncontrollably turned on by it. She said the only thing she didn't want was anything to do with shit, and that she preferred to cause pain with her bare hands rather than using an array of implements.

It wasn't up to me to say what I liked. I could acquiesce – or, of course, say that none of that was for me. I was beginning to realise that it all really might be. By this time, I was so wet, because she had touched me throughout the conversation in a proprietorial sort of way. I was tingly all over, and I could barely form words. She asked if I had any limits, and I said I was sure I did, but my imagination hadn't got that far yet. I told her that I was very inexperienced, to which she snorted and said I was clearly a complete slut whom she needed to take in hand.

We got some more drinks. The bar had filled up with a non-working cool crowd who apparently start their weeknights at 11 p.m.; the music was throbbing. Darla told me to stand up and come round to her side of the high table. I did. She made me spin round, and grabbed my arse. Then she spun me back to face her, saying, 'Not bad.' Then, with all the hipsters dancing around us, she theatrically undid my belt and my jeans, and pushed her hand inside my knickers. She leaned back in the chair and looked down at my exposed cunt, and said loudly, 'You're *so* wet. Why are you so wet?'

Some people looked round. I mumbled something.

'MISS!' she shouted. 'You ALWAYS call me Miss.' Then she told me to pick up our bags and drinks, before she grabbed my arm and dragged me up to a little mezzanine gallery. It was vaguely more private, but basically still visible to everyone on the floor below.

'Show me your clit,' she said.

I pulled down my trousers, and she pushed me onto a seat, facing out over the balcony. She roughly pushed her fingers into my cunt, and started thrusting hard. I felt like I might come immediately, and I cried out.

'Shut up,' she whispered. 'Spread your legs. I can't see anything.'

I spread my legs, feeling incredibly exposed up on the balcony, where everyone could see, if they happened to look up. I felt mortified that she could clearly tell that everything she had described wanting in a sub had aroused me so much that I was coming on the spot.

'You do have a very nice cunt,' she said, and I swelled with pride.

I was not allowed to come, but Darla wanted to. She told me she wanted me to lick her cunt till she came. She got up and, without letting me do up my trousers, took me downstairs to the basement. She dragged me into the graffiti-covered unisex toilets, and into a large cubicle with a door that was just about still on its hinges, but had a foot or so open below and above it.

'Sit,' she said, pointing to the fairly gross-looking toilet seat. I went to sit, but she said, 'Clean it first!'

So I wiped it with loo roll, really hoping she didn't have a fetish for making subs lick toilet seats. Then I sat down on the seat. Suddenly, as if she were a weirdly nimble Spider-Man sprite, her trousers and knickers were off, and she was straddling the cubical with her cunt just above my face.

'Look at my clit. LOOK AT IT. Tell me about it. You love it, don't you? You want to suck it?'

Through some kind of amazing acrobatics, every time I went to lick her, she moved just out of reach, till she made me beg to let my tongue connect with her swelling clit.

She told me exactly what to do to her, at the top of her voice, while a queue for the loos formed outside. She told me to suck her clit harder and harder, and to lick her all over, shouting 'Faster! Slower! Harder!' all the time. She grabbed my hair and looped it round her wrist and pulled my head back, shouting, 'Suck my clit, *harder*!' – but she was pulling my head back, so I couldn't reach her cunt. I kept trying to, but she was pulling my hair harder and harder in the opposite direction, at the same time shouting: 'Why aren't you sucking my clit? Suck it!'

Every time I leaned up to her, she would yank my hair down. I could feel my eyes watering and tears rolling down my cheeks. I really, really wanted to lick her cunt. I really wanted to make her come, but she wouldn't let me.

Finally, she relented and let go of my hair. Then, legs still bridged between the walls, she pushed her cunt down onto my face, pushing herself into me so I couldn't breathe. She continued shouted directions, telling me that she was going to come on my face. By this time, the people outside were knocking on the cubicle door in an irate fashion. Darla came, and I felt her cunt quiver next to my lips, my face wet and hot.

Like some kind of flexible hyena, she flipped down and stood, somehow fully dressed, looking down at me. 'Get dressed,' she said with disdain – though I only had undone trousers from earlier.

As I stood to zip up my flies, she pushed me roughly against the wall. She lifted up first one of my arms and then the other, holding them above my head. Pausing to yell at the waiting people in the queue that she would be done 'in two minutes', she then pulled my trousers down around my ankles, and stuck her long nails into my thighs, pushing them up onto my bum. Her nails were like razors. I screamed out, and she slapped me hard and said, 'SHUT UP.' She scratched me more and then spanked me hard, fully in earshot of the ever-growing queue.

Then she made me dress, and we left the cubicle. Darla marched ahead, head held high, dragging me by the wrist. The bemused punters' grumbles about us hogging the loo subsided in astonishment as we walked past.

'Don't you need to go now?' she said.

It was true, I begrudgingly realised; I needed to be home relatively early, before a busy day.

'When can you come to mine?' she asked. 'I'm free on Monday night.'

At this point, I probably would have sacked off all possible commitments to see her, so I agreed without even checking the diary. We said goodnight, though I think her night was only just beginning. I ran home feeling very horny and lucky, eager to tell Max all about it.

Getting off on fucking in public places is hardly unusual. In any crowded bar, in any city, you'll find horny dates sneaking off to the bathrooms together. It was recently reported that a beach in the Netherlands has had to erect signs threatening fines for getting it on in the sand dunes, as activity there had become so rife. The mile-high club is well populated, and if you walk down the High Line in New York and look up at the floor-to-ceiling windows of the Standard Hotel . . . you'll take my point. There is something so delightfully naughty, but not really that scary, about getting up to mischief in close proximity to the general populace. I suspect the people to whom this would not appeal in the slightest simply don't notice – they don't see the two girls pulling twigs from their hair and giggling as they emerge from behind some trees in a park. They don't notice the layer of sex permeating all life, like a shiver of kinky ghosts haunting the world, which only the specially attuned can see.

I think sometimes it is the sense of you and your partner together against the world that appeals when it comes to exhibitionism: the idea of being uninhibited, reckless, sexy and subversive. The dom/sub version of it – or at least the one Darla was playing with – is not so different, but the power is shifted so that the sub is the one being exhibited, humiliated, under the control of the dom, rather than the more mutual feeling of being the *enfants terribles* together. For the avoidance of doubt, both versions sound excellent to me.

❧

When I began to realise that the things that aroused me could be identified as 'submissive', I was annoyed at myself, and ashamed. Surely, as a woman, being 'dominant' is much better, and so much cooler. Wouldn't it be more feminist to get off on being in control, subjecting men to your will? I loved meeting female dominants – or femme doms or dommes (I think it's more gender neutral to write 'dom' for everyone, but some women – and by women, I mean anyone identifying as female – prefer 'domme' precisely for its feminine feel. The internet, on the other hand, loves 'femdom'.) I loved meeting them to submit to, but I also just loved hearing their stories – in the gendered world in which we live, the experience of being a female dom is different to that of being a male dom, and the experience of submitting to a woman is different for me.

My friend Erika's journey to realising she was a dom was like a reversed version of my life. As a child and teen, she strongly identified with and imagined herself into scenes involving a woman overpowering a man. She remembers rubbing herself raw to the scene in *Biloxi Blues* where Matthew Broderick's awkward young soldier character goes to empowered sex worker Rowena and she shows him what's what. As a tween, Erika imagined herself fully as Rowena, in a seat of sexual power with a young man as her plaything. In real life, she loved sucking her first boyfriend's cock while he was on the phone to his mum, having him completely in her power. With her first girlfriend, she assumed a dominant, in-charge, stereotypically 'male' role.

While I thought this all sounded much easier to live with than the feeling that you want to be subjugated, Erika said that she had experienced other issues. She was sure she wasn't feminine enough. She was too loud, too bossy, too assertive – she was bad at being a girl. As she began to have sex, she struggled to receive, and to let go of control; she only seemed to want to be in charge. This was often not OK with the men she dated, and clashed with their notions of what a girl should find hot.

The first time she experimented with an overt depiction of domination was with a boyfriend she had been seeing for several months. She suggested she would like to dress like a traditional dominatrix, and bought herself a riding crop. Although the role play seemed to work for them both, in the end he revealed he felt emasculated – not specifically because of the dom/sub role play, but because of how in touch she was with her own sexuality. That was intimidating for him, and made him feel jealous. Like she might go and threaten another man with her riding crop at any minute. I began to see, as she told me this, that there are a whole array of prejudices about dominant women.

Despite having played a little with scenes like this, Erika wouldn't have associated herself with BDSM and kink. She had no real interest in pain. She didn't really want to wear thigh-high boots and stub out cigarettes on prone men.

Eventually, a friend said to her, 'I really think you are a dom, and you should go and find some subs online.' Erika began to investigate. It wasn't smooth sailing. A lot of men she met who claimed to be subs were actually 'topping from below'. They had a wish list of events that they demanded the dom perform upon them. I hear about this again and again from femdoms: what they are seeking is the exquisite play of power in a connection between people, but what they get is a man wanting them to perform a vision of a fantasy, without showing any concern for the interplay or surrendering their power. This is a popular culture view of BDSM. Think of Jordan Belfort in *The Wolf of Wall Street* telling the sex workers what to do; it *looks* like the woman is a dominatrix, and she is causing him pain, but only strictly as he has demanded she does. The outfit is dictated by him and for his gaze. Erika might well get off on wearing a corset and heels if she fancies, but to be told to wear them is completely off-putting to her – whereas, for me, it would only be the *being told to* element that had any appeal.

A big difference in the way Erika and I identify with our kink roles is that for her, being dominant in sex and play feels like an extension of her personality. She is gloriously outspoken, authoritative, articulate and confident-seeming in normal life; she long ago came to terms with the fact that she is not a demure girly-girl wallflower. She trains hard and is physically strong – she could kick your arse. She's also – maybe ironically, as she never saw herself this way – an archetypal hot woman, with a tiny waist, curves, big eyes, full lips. She is a full-on superhero badass in real life, and her dom self is not so far away.

For me, by contrast, submission is totally remote from my day-to-day personality – which is one reason why it feels so arousingly subversive. Most of the male doms I know are more like me; they have absolutely no desire to control or dominate or cause pain in their normal lives. I wonder if, for Erika, it's different for two reasons. Firstly, she is not really into pain play; she likes playing with power and surrender, but she is not into caning people or sewing corsets into their backs. I think if you *are* into giving or receiving pain, it would be very difficult to see that as an extension of your regular personality – and if you did, you would, I hope, consider seeking help. Secondly, if Erika is dominating a man, it feels like a reversal of the patriarchy to her, and she feels very comfortable with that – whereas a male dom controlling a female sub could not feel like that without it being horrifying and misogynistic. Erika is queer, but she is usually only dominant with men. When she has sex with women, the role does not appeal so much, because it feels too much to her like the subjugation of women in real life. Fortunately for me, plenty of other femdoms do not feel that way. And perhaps that is because for them, their dom side feels nothing like their usual selves.

Erika is married to Tom. Max and I first met them at a sex party, where Max recognised Tom as the brother of a university friend. They had recently moved to the UK from the US, and were making friends in the kink scene. We were all wearing penguin onesies as the party had a Christmas theme, and Max had a broken leg and was there on crutches. All of this was highly amusing. We huddled into a decorative life-sized pâpier-maché igloo, the onesies came off, and we got to know each other better. The four of us played together in different variations and at different parties for years to come, and are firm friends, but the sexual relationship that has developed most is a dom/sub one between Tom and me. We have a very mutual interest in my being restrained and tied up to the beams of their warehouse ceiling, and in him pinning me down and fucking my brains out. Erika's other primary partner Jack is submissive, and loves her in her queenly dom role. She has a bell she will ring for him to come and attend to her. She told me he calls her 'Daddy' in a deep baritone, and it makes her immediately wet. Tom, Erika and Jack are 'fluid bonded' – which means they agree to have condom-free sex with each other and no-one else. Erika sometimes returns home to Tom from a date with Jack, still full of his come. Tom absolutely loves fucking her like this, feeling her cunt all stretched and full. Tom and Erika unleash their dominant sides with other very willing lovers, but it sounds like they have the most fun with just the two of them too.

❧

I woke up at about midday, feeling sticky and headachy and kind of horny in that hungover way. I looked ruefully at the empty space where Max should have been, cursing his work trip abroad. I knew if he had been here, and had been out last night with me, we would have spent the day slumping around and groping each other lazily. It would have been amazing. Instead, I settled into a day of not doing much, and soon Max and I were exchanging the filthiest messages. I was lying on the sofa with my vibrator, imagining all the things we were describing, feeling very turned on.

What did we *do* before text and WhatsApp? I remembered reading *The Sexual Life of Catherine M* and being so preoccupied by the logistics of the landline phone calls required to arrange liaisons. She seemed to be constantly having orgies out in the French countryside; was her assistant taking messages back at the office every time a suitor called? I love a long, chatty phone call – and I love phone sex. But it is kind of hard to schedule. Texts, on the other hand, can be read and sent surreptitiously in the office, or at dinner, or from a treadmill, and no one knows you're getting wet because someone just described something filthy they want to do to you. I have a friend called Abe – we will meet him later – whom I have only met in person once, because he lives in Austin, but we have escalated the kinkiness to an out-there degree over the course of a year, entirely through WhatsApp. Of course, it can also be easier to say what you want or like in text, in a way you might be too shy to say with your voice, or in person. It's a bit frustrating when people can't write well, or don't seem to see how fun and imaginative text message-based porn writing can be. I love a photo or a video, but I love words more, and I am so delighted when I find people I have met in person who, once we start to chat digitally, seem to enjoy co-imagining scenarios and describing them as much as me. I find it quite hard to sext people I've never met; I need to know who they are, their particular voice and personality, and be able to picture them in my mind doing whatever we are talking about. Sorry, AI, I don't think you'll ever get me off.

As Max and I continued to message, a notification appeared from Callum. We had met Callum recently for a drink. It transpired we had many mutual friends and shared interests. He was incredibly hot. Very muscular, tattoos all over his arms, short corn rows and a beautiful face – and, as we had discovered while chatting that evening, a very depraved mind. Sadly, we had not had a chance to meet up with him again since then, what with his and our travels.

Callum's message said, 'A little bird tells me you are worse for wear and desperate for some humiliation.'

Max had clearly messaged Callum and told him I was sitting at home alone feeling horny. I wondered if he had actually told him he should come round and put me out of my misery. The idea of Max sending men round to do unspeakable things to my body, without asking me, was always hugely arousing, as he well knew. I loved the way he was directing things from the other side of Europe, and the fact that he and Callum could be planning and plotting together made me deliciously scared and excited.

'I wonder how you could have heard such a thing!' I texted. 'I am very broken, but Max keeps telling me to do things, and now my cunt is a bit wet.'

Callum replied, 'Just as well he has got you in such a hole while I am on your side of town. It sounds like your cunt needs a throbbing cock to fill it.'

The conversation continued with some graphic descriptions of everything that would happen next. I was unsure whether he really was intending to come over or whether these were just messages – which I was very much enjoying anyway. I love the suspense you can build ahead of meeting. Most things, I think, are improved by getting extremely excited about them in the run-up. Max rolls his eyes about the packing lists I'll start making a month before a holiday, or how I will start thinking about outfits for festivals as soon as I buy the tickets. But I think everything is even better with anticipation, and sex is no different. And what a turn-on when someone arrives already hard or wet after hours or days of foreplay, all achieved with nothing more than words in little green boxes.

Callum told me I had to get up and get dressed and get ready for him. He told me to put on knee-high socks and a short skirt and a short top. Suddenly, my hangover felt much better, and I leapt into the shower. I dressed as he had instructed and sent him a picture to approve.

He asked for my exact address. When I gave it, by remarkable coincidence it transpired he was on my very street already. He said he was coming round, but was in the middle of something so could only visit briefly. He was basically going to come in, fuck me quickly, then leave again. I had worked myself up into a very horny state by this point. The thought that Max had basically dispatched a man to come and fuck me like this was agonising.

The doorbell rang and I buzzed Callum into the building. I heard him come up the stairs, and he knocked on the door. I answered, in my short white mini skirt, knee-high black socks and a bra. Without even saying hello, he grabbed me and kissed me hard, pushing me up against the hallway wall. He thrust his hand into my knickers; his fingers were cold and my cunt was so warm that the contrast felt amazing, making me cry out.

'You are so wet,' he said. 'You *really* need my cock, don't you?'

I could only nod; I was trembling and had lost the ability to speak.

He undid his trousers and pulled out his cock, and pushed my head down to examine it. It really was beautiful: smooth and very wide and very long. I began to suck and lick it. But soon he pulled me up and we tumbled into the bedroom. He bent me over the bed and pushed his fingers into me hard and fast and forcefully, even slightly brutally and painfully. After a day of thinking about being treated like this, for it to actually happen was almost too much, and I came in seconds. He pulled off his clothes and lay back on the bed, holding up his gigantic cock. His body was amazing, with beautiful tattoos all over his chest and back.

He said he wanted to see me gag. I didn't think this would be very difficult somehow. So I began to suck his cock and push it into my throat. My jaw felt like it would crack, and I could see stars as he pushed my head down further, choking me. Finally, as I was allowed up for air, he said he loved the feeling of me choking around his cock, my throat constricting as I struggled to breathe. Then he flipped me over onto my back and spread my legs. In one smooth motion, he pushed the whole of that huge cock deep into my cunt, making me gasp. I could feel my cunt clenching round his cock. I could feel seemingly every millimetre of it inside me. It was amazing. I grabbed his arse and pushed him even further in. He pinned down my hands and thrust harder and harder. Then I felt his cock shudder inside me as he came, and I felt my cunt spasming around it. I felt delirious.

After a couple of seconds, Callum got up and pulled on his trousers. 'Right,' he said. 'Well, that's all you're having for now, but there will be much more later. I expect you to be ready for me all evening, and for you to do exactly as I say. I'm at a wake across the road, but I'll leave it when I feel like it, with no warning.'

'You're at a *wake*?' I said. 'That is so wrong!'

At this, the dom roleplay thing did go a bit out the window, and we burst into laughter.

'It's fine, it's fine,' he said. 'The dead guy would totally have approved.'

Max is a very visual person. He loves photography. It was not surprising that he discovered there are many incredible photographers out there with a predilection for kink and BDSM, and that they are always seeking models for their work. This gave him an idea.

'But I'm absolutely shit at having my photo taken!' I protested. 'I'm not a model. I'll make a stupid face and be awkward!'

He replied that it wasn't about being a model, it was about him taking me somewhere and forcing me to strip naked in front of a stranger and do whatever humiliating things I was told to. I was reminded of the story 'Artists and Models' in Anaïs Nin's *Delta of Venus*. Anaïs is living in Greenwich Village and making money as a sculptor's model. She describes the sensation of being stared at, naked, but seen as a study, not as a sexual being – she feels like the clay being carved. At the time, she is also making ends meet by writing erotica for The Collector, who pays her a dollar a page. She is thus asking all her friends for erotic plotlines she can use. The sculptor starts telling her erotic stories while she poses naked for him. Still, this is supposedly an entirely professional, artistic encounter, not a sexual one. Mysteriously, his sculpture keeps getting sabotaged, and she has to go back again and again. Eventually, during one session, he moves across from the sculpture to touch her naked, posing her body as if it were the clay and he were moulding her. Of course, it ends in some typically steamy sex. It was one of my favourites of her works. Maybe modelling could be fun.

We met Derrick, who liked shooting tasteful art nudes, with the odd kinky twist. We met Sarah, who liked to tie me in beautiful shibari, then photograph that in a studio in an old church. We met Justin, who was a sci-fi geek, and made me pose as a naked stormtrooper. We met Wes, who took us out to an abandoned fertiliser factory and had me crawling naked in some probably quite toxic mud. Peter made me become a table, lying on my back balancing an extremely heavy glass sheet on my shins and hands, while people sat round placing drinks on it. Whether or not they identified as doms, or simply as creative directors, all the photographers took control, and I began to love being a part of someone else's visual fantasy and helping bring it to life. I liked having to be in awkward positions for hours on end, submitting to their will. I found it quite meditative, and would get into a trance-like state with no sense of time. If I was told to touch myself or fuck myself with a dildo or something, I figured, since I have no acting skills, it was better to go for it in reality, and I began to realise I loved being watched. It flipped between humiliation and exhibitionism, a line I have loved playing with ever since.

It was exciting to see how the pictures turned out, and it was lovely to build up a scrapbook. Max would use them on our profiles on the websites – this was before apps – which was then a great calling card for other photographers and playmates. I always thought I looked a million times better in this kind of picture, often prostrate, dirty and naked, than in 'normal' photos of me. Occasionally, Max would model too. One photographer wanted to shoot us fucking. We went to his studio, and there was a bed in the middle of it; we went for it, coyly at first, then with increasing abandon. The presence of a camera-wielding voyeur was extremely hot, we found.

In those early days of modelling, there was a clear boundary – the photographers might touch and tie and move my limbs, with my consent, but the shoots never turned into sex or play. I was a bit sad about that sometimes, but I felt uncomfortable about communicating that I might want more with photographers; I was unsure if it would be appropriate to suggest it. This whole world felt so new, and I was worried about getting things wrong or causing offence. I assumed, incorrectly, that all the other models a photographer would be working with were doing it simply for work – for payment, for their portfolios – not because they were uncovering a delicious new kink. As I tried more things, I noticed that a feeling comes first, then an attempt to define it to myself, and the ability and confidence to articulate and communicate to others, only so very much later.

I arrived in a flat the photographer Anthony had rented for the day. I had a slightly nervous *let's hope I don't get raped and murdered* feeling combined with excitement, a sensation that was increasingly familiar. I was becoming more confident about modelling, and about the trustworthiness of photographers, and Max had long since stopped escorting me. You would think that going to meet strange men and get naked in front of them would not feel safe, but it's surprising how soon you realise that most people *are* who they say they are. You can pick up on any bad vibes during the text chat, phone call and coffee meeting beforehand. Walking down a dark street feels much less safe than modelling for fetish photographers – and as a woman, you're statistically far more at risk at home with your husband.

Anthony welcomed me in. He was in his fifties maybe, very tall, with grey hair and a beard, and he had a vaguely louche, artistic air about him. I sat down and we talked about what he did, what the pictures were for, and what I wanted. As usual, I had to explain why someone not at all interested in becoming a professional model wanted to do this. I didn't go into how aroused it made me, but emphasised that it was for fun, and explained how much I loved his photos – they really were stunning, extremely atmospheric and beautiful.

I stressed that I needed to be directed a lot, and fortunately he said that was how he worked, with a very clear idea of what he wanted. That comment alone was enough to make me slightly aroused. While he was getting the cameras ready, he showed me some of his erotic photos. There was an amazing shoot on the Tube, with two naked girls basically doing porn on the Northern line. In one shot, there are other passengers asleep in the carriage. They did it at 5 a.m. when the Tube had just opened in a quiet area, but they did still end up getting told off by the transport police.

He showed me some where a girl had big welts on her bottom, and I asked if he had caned her. Anthony said yes, and told me he had brought his canes with him, just in case.

He asked me to get ready, telling me to remove all my clothes, and ushered me into a room to undress. I always thought it was quite funny how there is often a discreet changing area, even when you were about to be going full frontal. But I supposed it was professional, and to make people comfortable. I took off my clothes and folded them neatly. The canes comment played in my mind. That was clearly a suggestion. Would I do that? I decided to see what happened.

I came back out into the main room naked, feeling a bit self-conscious and not sure what to do with my arms.

Anthony said, 'Can I just check that you haven't got any marks from your clothes or anything?' and proceeded to examine my body in close detail while I stood in the middle of the room. Being studied like this was somehow both humiliating and exhibitionist; it was remarkable how this simple activity of him looking closely at me had introduced a power dynamic, one that went much further than the photographer/model relationship. I reflected how, in another instance, the act of gazing at someone could be worshipful and more submissive. So often, it's not *what* you're doing, but *how* it's being done, I was learning. Anthony did not have a worshipful and submissive air – not at all.

We started with some fairly tame shots, art nude style. Then we graduated to more adult ones, with me kneeling over things and spreading my legs, or putting a hand between them. Increasingly, I noticed the shots were taking on a more submissive feel. Simple poses, like me kneeling down with my head bowed or my hands behind my back. Anthony seemed to be happiest with these. I wondered if that was because I was better at modelling those poses, as they came more naturally, or because he was a dom who enjoyed seeing them.

After a few of these shots, he asked me outright if I was a submissive.

I still had a kind of imposter syndrome about describing myself as a submissive to highly experienced BDSM practitioners. While I knew my mind could go fully sub, there were so many things I had never tried, or even heard of.

And if I answered yes, what did that mean about the canes?

Pain was interesting. My secret submissive fantasies, before I ever started sharing them, had tended to be much more about humiliation. If I imagined being tied to a ship's mast and flogged (thanks, *Hornblower*), I wasn't fantasising about the feeling of the whip destroying my skin; it was more about the people watching it happen to me. I think it is more difficult to fantasise a physical feeling than a psychological one, especially if you have never had the experience in real life. As I had learned more about the kink world, I had discovered there was a difference, and I wasn't sure if I was really into physical pain. I liked a spank or a slap, a twist of a nipple, a choke, a hair pull – but was this just because of the power dynamic these things symbolised, not the pain itself? I had enjoyed the kind of dominant sex where my cunt or arse were pounded and stretched in a painful way. Max was getting more confident with his floggers. I had come back from plenty of kinky nights proudly bruised, but still, I was not sure if I could ever be one of those submissives I had seen subjected to pure pain, not as a part of sex, and clearly receiving something secret and magical from it in its own right.

I had thought a little about real-life pain. I get migraines; the kind that, as a child, would see me sent to A&E with suspected meningitis. These started with psychedelic auras heralding a white, fiery pain and then overwhelming nausea, which as a teenager could last for a few days. All the women in my family have them. The medical profession has little to offer sufferers, but the wisdom of women does. I loved Siri Hustvedt's migraine-suffering characters, and indeed her writing about her own. She made me feel that the strange lights were a gift, almost a portal into another way of seeing the world. More pragmatically, my mother had taught me not to panic. I had come to learn that for me, some of the pain and most of the nausea could be avoided if I really focused when the aura first began to alter my vision, trying to calm my breathing, relax and accept what was happening. If I could stem the tide of adrenaline, this seemed to lessen the pain.

As a child, I had been obsessed with ballet. Traditional ballet teaching has a distinctly sadistic streak, and I wonder how much this might have contributed to my desires. The coupling, from age three onwards, of beauty and art with physical pain – maybe this had embedded itself deep in my psyche. My fellow dance students and I would compete over whose toes were the bloodiest, and who could keep jeté-ing the longest when our thighs were burning and our hearts were beating fit to burst. Ballet is permeated with the sense of physical sacrifice in pursuit of transcendence. Causality is hard to prove, though – did I love ballet *because* it was tapping into some innate submissive tendencies, or did it give them to me? Or are they unconnected? Perhaps I am finding links purely because humans like patterns. I do not think the majority of ballet students go on to become masochistic perverts, after all.

I answered Anthony's question nervously and equivocally. 'Er . . . I think so.'

He looked at me for what felt like an age without saying anything. I was still kneeling naked before him and he was standing, towering over me, holding his camera. He was very still. 'I think you are too.'

Over the years, when I got to know Anthony much better, I would come to learn that he is amazing at creating a mood, or 'holding space' as meditation teachers would say. It's a real art. He went to a Jesuit school, attending an elaborate, incense-filled high church Mass every morning. In general, I think it is reductive to connect childhood religious practices with adult fetishes. Dr Lehmiller and other psychologists suggest that if you live within a system of strict moral codes – for example, those of religion or right-wing 'family values' orientated politics – this sometimes encourages you to rebel, and your kinky desires can be a product of that; they feel even more transgressive and exciting. I am sure that might be true in some cases, but it feels like a minority. Catholics are certainly not all out at Munches after Mass. It would be interesting to learn whether the least permissive of societies have a higher or lower percentage of kink lovers than others. I suspect it would be the same as in any other group – from our small, unscientific sample, it feels like kink people come from every conceivable walk of life you could imagine.

In my case, although Bible stories might have been some of the earliest stories I heard, I quickly found submissive narratives in many other places, and I don't think the Bible stories caused my daydreams; they were just what my brain had to work with before Nancy Friday gave me group sex and the neighbour's dog. My parents' version of Christianity didn't stress sexual rules and regulations. They were early backers of Church-sanctioned gay marriage, and they didn't put any pressure on me or my sister to marry and have children. They didn't talk about sex much, and to this day I have no idea how I could possibly broach the topic of kink and consensual non-monogamy, but I think this has more to do with their middle-class baby-boomer culture than their religion.

I think what Anthony and I might have been bequeathed by the Church, though, is an appreciation of theatre. How you move and speak, the space around you, the sounds, the smells: all can be choreographed to create a feeling of something beyond normal experience. In church, you are supposed to connect that feeling with access to the divine. When you're watching Shakespeare, it is art. At a rave, the DJ curates euphoria. In yoga, you're reaching for *samadhi* – pure bliss. Understanding from such a young age how we, ordinary people, can work together using ritual to create transcendence: maybe this is a contributing factor to what we both searched for in sex. (Years later, when I suggested this to him, Anthony shrugged. He thinks everything contributes, that our minds are each a unique tapestry of experience, and that we can't know which specific aspects made us how we are; he thinks it is entirely down to the blending and processing. The wine is not the wine only because of the grape.)

I knew something had shifted emotionally in this photoshoot, and I knew I was excited about it. But I was unsure how to transition a shoot into play, I wasn't quite confident enough to voice the thought. But if Anthony was going to suggest that the session moved from purely photography to something more, I was very curious and willing to see what that might entail.

'If you would like to try, I would like to cane you, and I would like to photograph the marks. I am very good at it. It will look beautiful. And I think you might like it.'

I somehow loved that his primary concern was seemingly aesthetic. It was as if he was appealing to my sense of 'anything for art!' – much as my childhood ballet classmates had compared our bleeding toes. But there was something about the way he seemed sure I would like it, or at least be intrigued enough to try; I felt like he could see through my external personality into some dark, pain-loving kernel within, and that *this* was his real field of expertise.

I said I was very, very scared, but yes, I would like to try.

He nodded. He put down his camera and brought out a long, hard case, which looked like it would contain a musical instrument. Instead, it contained about five long canes. They were various widths and lengths. Some were smooth, and some had knots.

He told me to stand up and bend over the table. He gently moved my arms and my legs into the exact position he wanted, it was like being adjusted into the correct form in a yoga class, a touch both kind and professorial. I realised I was already gripping the edge of the table and my knuckles were white.

The first stroke was a huge shock. The sound was ear-splitting and I felt the pain ripple through my body. I was suddenly hot and clammy all over, and could feel the adrenaline coursing through me. I straightened up in shock.

'No,' he said calmly. 'Four more. You are fine.'

Somehow, my body acquiesced.

The second stroke felt like it landed in exactly the same place as the first. I really thought I was going to cry, but I think I just screamed and managed not to stand up, pressing my face into the hard table.

The strokes came too quickly for my mind to process. I was not consciously thinking *You can do this*, or *Don't ask him to stop*, or *You must please him*, or any conscious thoughts at all, but some deep survival mechanism kicked in, alongside a clear masochism, and my body stayed in place of its own accord to receive what he was giving.

After the fifth stroke, I heard him put down the cane. I felt his eyes on my arse.

'They are going to look brilliant.' He reminded me of a TV chef: *Mmm, this thing I just made is so delicious, I'm so talented.*

He took my hand and lifted me up, looking into my eyes. 'You did really, really well. How do you feel?'

I was trembling all over, but I was aware that while my arse stung a bit, it didn't really hurt. What was going on in the rest of my body was a different matter. I felt different, as if unknown chemicals were racing around my bloodstream. This was a completely new experience for my mind and body. I wasn't perceiving it as good or bad, I was simply fascinated. I had assumed that all I would feel was pain, and it would just be about how much I could endure. But there was so much else going on. I felt like new synapses were growing in my brain. I once tried to argue with a friend who was reluctant to try magic mushrooms – he was convinced that he would be so anxious, he would be unable to enjoy them. I tried to explain that part of the experience of the mushrooms was that they made you relaxed and happy, so he would be less anxious than normal (I backed down when I realised it's not OK to try to persuade people to take drugs . . .). I wondered if something similar was going on here; something about the overall effect on my brain had mitigated the pain.

'Come here,' Anthony said, and enveloped me in a big hug for a minute or two, stroking my hair until I stopped shaking.

He got me a glass of water, and showed me the cane he had been using. It was broad, long and solid. I held it reverentially, marvelling that I had survived being hit with it.

When he could see I was fine, and I had begun to talk normally again, he said we had to take photos of the marks. First, he took me to a mirror so I could see. I looked over my shoulder and had to agree with him: they were beautiful. There were three neat lines on each cheek. The cane had evenly landed on both sides, with two of the strokes exactly on top of the other. They were a bright, deep red. The blood was drawn so close to the surface, it made me feel even more like my deepest insides were being pulled out into the light.

He picked up his camera again, and started to shoot me from angles that showed off the cane marks. Once or twice he asked to touch them, and when I consented he squeezed them, presumably in a way that made them stand out more for the pictures. When he did this, the stinging turned to a deeper, bruising sensation, and something new switched on in my brain again.

We finished, and I went into the little room to get dressed. In my jeans and T-shirt, smudged mascara wiped off, I knew there was no external sign of what strange shifts might have just taken place in my body's chemistry. But I had a strange sense that this was a beginning, and life might never be quite the same again.

I walked home across London Bridge. My jeans rubbed against my developing welts. As I paused and looked over the Thames, I realised that my cunt was absolutely pulsing. *Pain*, I thought. *Interesting*.

The cane marks faded. First their neat edges blurred, then the bruises turned purple, then green, yellow, brown, until eventually they disappeared. But the sound of the crack, the surge of adrenaline, and the strange gratitude I'd felt to Anthony: none of that had faded from my mind. I would find myself suddenly, viscerally, reliving it all throughout the day. Anthony asked if I wanted to shoot again, and how I felt about the caning. I said I felt like a whole new door of perception had been opened, and I wanted to step through it. The conversation moved beyond photography and modelling, and I knew, as we made plans to 'shoot' again, that what he was really inviting me to was something else entirely.

I cycled up to the address Anthony had given me. It was a beautiful and very grand street, and as I locked my bike and knocked on the door of an eighteenth-century townhouse, I wondered if this was where he lived or if he had borrowed it for the shoot. Anthony answered the door and I kissed him hello. I was hyperactive and chatty; he was his more laconic, calm self.

We had cups of tea and he showed me the house, which he had bought a year ago as a complete wreck and had very lovingly restored. I didn't know who, if anyone, lived with him there. It was filled with beautiful antique furniture. The dining room had a long banqueting table. There were stone steps down to a cellar. It felt like being on a film set. I kept remembering *The Story of O* – in my mind, the mysterious house she is taken to is furnished a lot like this. There is something about old houses – or castles, or churches – that is just quite fetish. I get the whole modernist mid-century obsession, but clean lines and Eames chairs just don't suggest drama, mystery, storytelling and magic in the same way. It made sense that Anthony's house had a palpable sense of history and buried secrets, and it made me feel like I was in a play, only I had no idea what the script would say.

We went into a first-floor sitting room, with original, dark wood floorboards and beautiful Georgian furniture. He showed me some pictures from recent shoots of his, and we talked about photography in general for a bit. Abruptly, he said, 'I think you need to take off all your clothes now.' I understood immediately that we were now playing, and it was as if a switch had been flicked in my brain, automatically accessing a different kind of behaviour. I was always amazed at how a word, a touch, a change in demeanour could palpably switch the normal world into something which looked the same, but with completely different energy – like a less scary Upside Down in *Stranger Things*. I got undressed. He asked if I had brought heels with me. I had: my very high, strappy red Vivienne Westwood shoes. He made me put them on. Somehow, I already felt very exposed sitting on the floor in front of him, naked, doing up the buckles while he looked impatient. He then asked me to stand up in the middle of the room. He walked round me, looking at my body, and then ran his hands over my waist and bottom.

'You have lots of marks from your clothes,' he said. Speaking quietly but clearly critically, he established his authority immediately. I wanted to please him, but I felt like I had already disappointed him and done something wrong. And I knew that he wanted me to feel like this. Our roles were assigned and I was acquiescing to mine, submitting to it, and to him. It didn't really matter what I was being chastised for. It never does; picking a fault is like a MacGuffin, something to move the plot along.

He directed me to an antique chair by a sash window overlooking the street. I noticed a few people walking by, who would possibly be able to see in.

'Sit in the chair. Lean back. Now spread your legs.'

He took photos with the light from the window falling over my body. He directed me in minute detail, dictating exactly how I should move my body, which was useful as I still had little actual modelling capability. I was already feeling turned on by being nakedly subjected to his will like this, and the sense of his attention and critical eyes all over me was feeling very hot – part humiliation, part exhibitionism, that perfect sweet spot between the two that I was coming to find so arousing. He was very tactile, moving my limbs into position and stroking me, ostensibly to see if the marks on my skin from my clothes had gone down, but, I suspected, really to assert his control over and ownership of my body. We did some shots seated and standing, and some with me bending over, touching my toes and arching my back. Anthony constantly stroked and moved me, saying, 'You have the ideal body for this,' in a way that was somehow both complimentary and menacing.

After lots of these, he said he wanted to take some rope shots. He made me kneel down on the floor in front of him, and told me to press my face into the floor next to the fireplace, with my knees spread and feet together, arse in the air, and arms between legs, with my hands next to my feet. He then took out the ropes and tied my wrists to my ankles. It's a very helpless position to be in. I was conscious that he was going to be photographing my cunt, and I knew that it would already be red and glistening wet, and he would be able to see this. He pushed me forward so my face was closer to the fireplace . . . and for some reason, I thought this would be a good moment to ask if the fireplace was original, which was an absurd thing to say given my position, and we both collapsed into fits of giggles. At least, I collapsed as much as it is possible to when your hands are tied to your ankles and your face pressed into a hearth.

After several shots like this, Anthony untied me and told me to stand up in the middle of the room again. He went to get the long box, which I now knew contained his canes. My heart started beating like crazy. Knowing what to expect this time made the anticipation even greater. I began to sweat, and could feel adrenaline coursing through my body in a delicious, excited way. He opened the case slowly and took something out, then walked back to me. He lifted my chin up with his hand, and shook his head. 'Not yet; something else first.'

He took out two clothes pegs. He pulled my left nipple and twisted it so roughly that I cried out. It was a sharp pain, but it simultaneously released a wave of endorphins. I fleetingly thought, *How does this work? Why does this pain feel so good?* But I couldn't dwell on it. He slapped my breast hard, and then attached the peg. It was big and wooden, with tightly coiled springs. It was an ecstatic agony. People had bitten or pulled on my nipples before during sex, which I had liked but not found particularly exciting, but this was next level. The intensity was turning my innocent nipple into an extra clitoris. It was as if a direct pathway between it and my cunt had been activated. I thought I might immediately gush onto the heritage floorboards.

When my breathing had returned to normal, he suddenly flicked the peg on my left nipple hard, and then attached the other one to my right nipple. I was crying out with emotion – I couldn't really distinguish whether it was pain or pleasure, it was like a brand new chemical my brain had made, for which I did not have a name. The more I cried, the more he pulled and twisted the pegs, making it more extreme. Later I came to learn that Anthony, like many other doms, is great at responding to what he sees. I know that he was delighted this was working on me, and he could tell it was new for me, and that's why he was upping the intensity. I know that even without me saying anything, he would have been able to tell if it was unpleasant or indeed boring for me. If that had been the case, he would have moved on.

He took out the camera and took lots of shots, stopping to pull and tweak the pegs, taking them off and putting them on again. He began to slap my face, too, with the front and back of his hand, causing the blood to rush to the skin and tears to prick my eyes and fall down my cheeks. He was taking photos in between, and I loved how I couldn't pose – I was too overcome and aroused. I couldn't try to arrange my face or stiffen like I might normally in the presence of a camera; I felt he must be capturing something real and authentic. Indeed, these early photos of his are some of my very favourites. I look so wide-eyed, wild and abandoned.

He said I was writhing around too much, so he forced me to my knees and tied my hands behind my back; I felt even more vulnerable and exposed, and this connected in my mind to the millions of humiliation fantasies I had imagined over the years. I realised it was as if I had been mentally practising for this since I was five years old.

At this point Anthony, very seriously, and like a gentleman, stopped and pointed out that this shoot may have become more about play than pictures. He wanted to double-check I was definitely happy with this. I was already in some kind of pain-adrenaline-endorphin-fuelled submissive hell-heaven, so unsurprisingly I was, indeed, fine with this. I was really marvelling that there was a real-life person who would go to the same extremes as the phantoms in my mind. He seemed to know my body better than I did, like a massage therapist who spots knots you could not have identified yourself. At this point, I was too involved in my own discovery of all these new feelings to wonder what he was getting out of it. As time went on, and I heard more about what doms are feeling too, I became increasingly amazed about the perfectly tessellating interaction; how my submission and his dominance were working together.

His eyes sparkled evilly. 'OK, bend over. Hands on the sofa.'

I saw him take out the largest cane. I was shaking all over. The first stroke came, and I felt it in every single cell. I felt faint, and was shrieking and writhing around, but every fibre of my being still screamed *more*.

'Stay. Still,' he commanded. Otherwise, he was completely silent. Four more cracks followed. I knew that I needed to lean in to the feelings, the intensity. Trying to mitigate, to escape, to move – although your conscious mind tells you to – will only prevent the wonderful systems that are actually protecting you from kicking in. It is the surrender and acceptance that make the pain break through the barrier and into something sublime. I did not think this consciously in the moment – I only articulated it to myself much later – but even now, at this second-ever caning, I think I had an instinctive and automatic grasp of this strange, beautiful concept.

This did not mean I managed to stay still and be calm; far from it. But although I spasmed crazily with each stroke, mentally I was not trying to escape. I was submitting.

When he let me stand up, I just wanted to be held. I think he could tell; he hugged me and stroked my hair, and said I was brave. The surge of love I had for him in that moment was far beyond conscious thought. He was so still and calm. My pulse was racing and my skin was tingling. He was fully clothed and quite smartly dressed; I was naked and bruised. Somehow, this was so exquisite. It was so real. I was not acting, seeking compliments, or pretending to be grateful, or like I needed his comfort as a role; it was an authentic response. It was extremely intimate.

He made me lie face down, and we did a large number of shots to highlight the cane marks. I was tied up in various ways, and had the pegs reattached to my now slightly bleeding nipples. Often, before taking the picture, Anthony would spank the cane marks with his hand to make them stand up even more.

After some time, Anthony said I could have a break, and invited me to kneel on the floor in front of the sofa.

He asked if I wanted a drink. I had no idea how much time had passed since I'd arrived at 11 a.m., but I thought alcohol was definitely allowed given the circumstances. He brought me a glass of wine and fed it to me. We then had a pretty normal conversation, considering I was sitting naked except for red heels, at his feet, covered in cane marks, with bleeding nipples and red cheeks, while he reclined on the sofa above me. We discussed *The Master and Margarita*, as he was currently reading it, and which Russian authors we liked, and whether 'Nabokov' has the stress on the first, second or third syllable. It was triggering my well-worn 'university tutorial' fantasy in a big way.

After the wine, I finally stopped shaking, and felt slightly more grounded. And tipsy – as well as the effects of all the adrenaline, I had only eaten a hot cross bun all day. When Anthony could see I was more recovered, he said it was time for more marks to be made on my body. I looked incredulous.

'Oh, you can take more,' he said. I believed him. Aside from the role of authority he had assumed, I genuinely trusted his expertise. It was so clear he knew what he was doing. Nothing was accidental; he was deeply focused. He knew this was all new for me, but I also felt a prickle of pride that I must be doing quite well if I was capable of more.

He bent me over again. The first crack came, and I wriggled and cried out.

'No,' he said. 'You do *not* move between strokes.' He quickly made several more strokes of increasing strength. Then, before I could stand up, he pushed me onto the floor, face down, and tied up my hands and feet. We took more photos in variations of this position – he would move me around by kicking me with his feet.

Then he decided I could have more wine. Again, I was kneeling on the floor in front of him, and he fed it to me, pulling my hair back roughly and tipping the wine into my mouth. And then he put his thumb into my mouth, pressing it down firmly onto my tongue. He pushed his fingers deep into my mouth, far down my throat, so I was choking. It was such a visceral reference to having a cock forced deep into my throat. When he lifted my head and said, 'Good girl,' I felt myself imagining his cum on my face. My cunt was throbbing. I looked down at the floor.

'Can't you look me in the eyes anymore?' Anthony asked, and lifted my head up. He looked at me with an expression that clearly said, *I have total power over you right now; I know this, you know this, you are mine.*

He went back to the box of canes. He took out a smaller one.

'No, no, I can't . . .' I said.

'Don't worry, your bottom is fine. Now turn and face me, and put your hands on your head.'

I think my poor addled brain took some time to work out what was coming, and the first 'thwack' across my stomach was a shock. He worked quickly, up and down the fronts of my thighs and torso, often going over the same spots with two strokes. It was hugely painful – and somehow I had never thought of being caned anywhere other than my arse. Though the cane was thinner, it was 'whippier', and had a huge sting. When he hit my stomach, I felt like my organs were all vibrating inside me. It was such an odd sensation, and I was finding it so interesting. Different places produced such different effects – the closer to my cunt, the more it pulsated. I would come to love being caned on an inner thigh perhaps the most of all. But being caned on my stomach and breasts felt like an offering. I felt a bit like a sacrificial medieval maiden tied to a tree. I'm not sure if Anthony would have been the rescuing knight or the dragon.

He made me lie down on my back and took pictures of his handiwork, examining the marks and running his hands over them, admiring his accuracy. If I relaxed, he pressed into them, causing my pulse to race again. He looked at me with a raised eyebrow, then moved my hand and put it on my cunt, which was dripping so much there were wet patches on the floor. He looked me in the eyes as I began to touch myself, which felt like an amazing relief. I thought I would come in three seconds, but he quickly brushed my hand away.

There were more ropes and tying into strange positions, and more pegs on my nipples. When I accidentally flinched and moved back from the peg as he tried to attach it, he took out a riding crop, and hit my inner thighs with it as a punishment. He put rubber bands round the pegs to make them tighter. He held on to the pegs and said I had to pull them off myself by leaning away from him, tugging my nipples out. If I didn't, he would make them tighter and tighter, and it would hurt even more. I couldn't do it. I seemed to be able to accept pain from him but, at this point, actively causing it when told to was beyond me. I thought, *I wonder if I will be able to do this one day*. I was already seeing this as a first lesson, and instinctively knew there would be many, many more.

He relented, and pulled the pegs off together, violently, taking chunks of skin with them.

We did more photos, with me in abject and humiliating poses. I was face down on the floor with my legs spread out when the doorbell went.

'Stay there,' Anthony said, and I heard him go downstairs. I heard the sound of the front door being opened, and muffled voices. Then, I was rather shocked to hear two pairs of footsteps coming up the stairs. I went to look up as I heard the feet come into the room.

'No, face the floor. You can only look when I say so.'

The other person was clearly in the room too, seeing me naked, my wet cunt visible, and my body caned all over. I wondered what was going on.

Then I heard another voice, Australian, female: 'Oh my god. What have you *done* to her?'

'This is Nicky,' said Anthony. 'No – stay down there. Do not turn your head.'

The hardest thing, actually, was ignoring a long-ingrained impulse to politely introduce myself to a person arriving in a room.

Nicky, it turned out, was another model of Anthony's. She had said she would stop by to collect some prints, and Anthony had clearly decided to orchestrate this as another way to assert his control and humiliate me. She, however, was not a sub, but usually shot with him in a dominatrix role.

As they chatted, I was not allowed to move from my prone position. Nicky approached me on the floor, and gently stroked me all over.

Anthony offered her a drink and they both sat down on the sofa. He beckoned me over and made me bend over his lap. He then spanked me with his hands, going hard over all the caning marks. Nicky pulled my hair and ran her hands gently over my back as he was doing this. It felt amazing; her soft skin and gentleness after and alongside all the violence was a very heady combination. I loved seeing how Anthony was with a female friend and model who was not his sub – it was completely different, and reinforced the conviction that it was my willing submission to him, and my enjoyment, which aroused his desire to dominate. Without that component, he would be absolutely uninterested in having power over someone.

In the years to come, I would hear this again and again from heterosexual male doms, when I was curious about how they came to find this side of themselves. Almost always, a woman had expressed their submissive fantasies, and the dom had found something incredible in enacting them.

After taking more photos, we realised it was nearly time to stop. Anthony said he had enough material, and handed me a glass of wine. I went to stand up and put a jumper on, but he looked at me and said, 'No, you kneel there.'

So Nicky and Anthony sat clothed on the sofa while I knelt naked on the floor, as we talked about what Nicky was up to.

Eventually, Anthony said, 'OK, you can sit by me now.'

I got up and sat between them on the sofa. They both stroked me, on my face, and my back and thighs, and Anthony said I had done very well. He kissed me on the forehead and said I could get dressed.

I put my clothes on, and then said goodbye to Nicky. Anthony took me downstairs to show me out; we hugged like normal people and both said we had had a lot of fun. I went out into the afternoon, and cycled home, standing on the pedals all the way, as I couldn't sit on the saddle, wondering how on earth I would survive the foursome Max and I had planned with Ian and Ellie in only an hour's time – but that's another story.

❧

At the time I met Anthony, and when Max and I were beginning our adventures, the mainstream media and social media were apparently yet to learn the word 'consent'. You would not hear the concept even expressed in normal conversation. In the kink universe, however, both the word and what it really means were one of the main topics of conversation. Whereas heteronormative, regular dating culture had yet to see that lunging in for an unasked-for snog or butt-grab may be assault, the kink universe had become more aware precisely *because* some of the practices look, from the outside, like things mainstream culture already considered problematic. The irony is that consensual flogging, for example, might *look* more like assault than non-consensual groping, which actually *is* assault. Because of the extreme nature of some of these practices, it was more obvious, maybe, that clear consent needed to be granted, and people had thought a lot about how to ensure this was happening.

In many ways, consent is easier to navigate when you are in a codified space, especially one geared towards sexual and fetish play. If you are at a ticketed event, you will have signed up to a code of conduct, and in order to get their licence, the venue will have to have put in place strict rules, and anyone flouting them has to be ejected. This is not the case in regular clubs or bars – even today (it should be!). If you are making one-on-one arrangements, you have to discuss what you are planning to do in advance – when does this ever happen on 'regular' hook-ups or dates? The honesty that's required to say, 'Yes, I do like water sports, but I do not like scat play,' tends to put you in a place of clear communication from the outset.

However, I wondered, as I went to meet more doms, and the activities began to involve more restraint and more pain, how would I, in the moment, communicate if something was wrong? What if suddenly it all got too much? How would they know the difference between role-play submission and me really feeling like I needed an out? How could I trust them? Sometimes, at first, doms would give me safe words. One, I remember, said it had to be my mother's name, which I suspect was more his 'thing' than mine, but was amusing – kinkifying the safe-word process. But now, I tend to feel that if we need a safe word, we do not have the appropriate level of communication on all levels to be doing what we are doing. I only want to surrender to people I trust so entirely, that if I said simply and seriously, 'Actually, can we stop now?', they would.

Anthony laughed once when we were discussing this. 'Consent? That doesn't even *begin* to cover it. I do not need only consent, or even "enthusiastic positive consent"; I need to know that the submissive is going to have a fully transcendental experience, that this experience is deeply important, that their trust is absolute, and that we have an intimacy and connection. Of *course*, if anything changed second by second, and they were no longer happy to do what we were doing, we would stop. But we would stop long before that if it wasn't amazing, too. The aim is not for the sub to be just "OK".'

I am not suggesting that the kink universe and BDSM culture is a utopia free from all misunderstanding, harassment, prejudice and sexual assault. I have certainly heard stories about submissives using masochism as self-harm, and I have heard about an alleged rape at a sex party. There must be predators posing as doms. And there must be uneducated, misogynistic, transphobic or homophobic people in these communities, as elsewhere. I have personally witnessed a person at a small party paying just too much attention to another, when it was clearly unwanted. He was kicked out. Apps and websites aimed at the kink world are as likely to have idiots, trolls and fakers as the internet all round.

But whereas I have frequently experienced non-consensual touch and have been made to feel uncomfortable at work events, in bars, at clubs and at house parties, and have experienced such unwelcome attention from strangers, professional contacts, acquaintances and even friends, I have never encountered this in the context of a kink event. Ordinary public space often doesn't feel safe, and I am a cis, white, middle-class woman living in a reasonably liberal Western city; ordinary public space must feel – and is – even less safe for members of marginalised communities, and in other places. For its participants, I think the kink world can often provide a way to be yourself free from the fear sadly present in the everyday world.

In fact, long before 'everyone was talking about it', I would look at things happening at a 'vanilla' party – or, indeed, on the Tube – and be very aware of threatening, predatory behaviour making people uncomfortable, and yet still being accepted as the norm. I think this was because I was having to think about it in so much detail, and having so many conversations about it. Many other people who are into BDSM have said the same. I hope that today the kind of discussions on consent I was having in my late twenties because I was trying to find out if I would like to be suspended from the ceiling and flogged, are now happening in primary schools as basic sex education.

I have never stopped proceedings because of the intended pain – I like playing with the edge too much, and I think the doms are usually more worried about me than I am – but I have had to because of physical discomfort: a cramping leg, a too-numb hand, feeling slightly too dizzy from something around my neck. I think this mirrors the emotional reasons I have ever called a halt, too – I have never done so from feeling threatened or unsafe, but I have if I'm feeling a bit bored, or just not aroused. Someone once told me, 'Life is too short for a bad French fry.' When there are such excellent French fries out there, why keep eating any that are just OK?

You can stop, at any moment, for any reason whatsoever, and so can whoever you are playing with, in whatever role. No explanation is needed, and no offence should be taken. If I have any doubts at all about that being the case, I do not proceed.

As a kid, my nickname was Tigger. Whatever strange fantasies my night brain might have given me, during the day, I bounced around, climbing on people I liked, which was everyone, and jumping up and down with enthusiasm about everything, and on top of everything, leaving a trail of broken furniture in my wake.

At some point, I learned this was deeply uncool. As a teenager in the nineties, being cool was everything. First, you should not be enthusiastic about school, because then you would be a swot. Then, you should not be enthusiastic about many genres of music, because they were lame (such genres included classical music, musical theatre and boy bands). Then, when boys came onto the scene, the ultimate cultural decree was that to be *keen* was suicide. If you were clearly DTF, you were a slut. The way to ensnare your man, which was what we clearly wanted to do as seventeen-year-old girls, was to be *chased*. You should never call first, never put out on the first date. Our idol Kate Moss said, 'Never complain, never explain.' The coolest thing was to be enigmatic, beautiful and largely silent.

This helpful cultural rulebook was overlaid by my deciding that, rather than attending a comprehensive school in a small suburban town, I actually lived on the Left Bank of Paris in the sixties. I was Simone de Beauvoir, infinitely French, sexy and cool. I manifested this by smoking filterless Gitanes and drinking absinthe (both of which made me quite ill), wearing a lot of eyeliner, and dressing in oversized, dark-coloured men's shirts from Oxfam. I tried my best not to smile.

None of this, unsurprisingly, made me feel good. If someone desired 'cool, nonchalant Sonnet', it only reinforced my belief that 'really keen Sonnet' was undesirable. And since no one saw the 'real' Sonnet, I had no data to suggest that people might desire her. But if I was rejected, with the logic of what must be a near-universal teenage-girl brain, I assumed that was down to the *real* me's failure – even though I was trying my best not to show her to anyone. So, in the most pointless feedback loop, I kept trying to be more like I was not, acting out whatever I thought sexy and cool was – which certainly wasn't boundless enthusiasm.

One of my biggest epiphanies, which should be blindingly obvious, but around sex – and particularly for women – is not, is that *people like enthusiasm*. Not fake-orgasm enthusiasm, but genuinely expressing it when you are up for stuff, making invitations, and showing you're having a good time when you are, in fact, having a good time.

I was feeling very . . . well-disposed towards a friend called Jimmy. As I had got to know him better, I'd learned he was even more of a joyously out-there loon than I had realised, and I loved it. I kept telling him how much I liked him, and we had hooked up a couple of times. He lived far away, so logistics were not easy. One day, he mentioned he was in town, but only for meetings. I was working from home, and I suggested that he came round, even if just for half an hour, to put me out of my misery. He was non-committal; I was *extremely* keen, and mentioned this repeatedly. I had no idea if he would show up, but I was making myself very overexcited at the thought he might. Happily, he decided he had a brief window. I opened the door in a little slip dress and nothing else, and we made it as far as the hallway. I pretty much came as soon as he touched my cunt, and within minutes his cock, hard on arrival, was in my mouth. We tumbled into the bedroom and had the kind of urgent, fast fuck that some afternoons are made for.

'Fucking hell,' he said afterwards. 'I've never seen a cunt so wet and someone quite so up for it. It's absolutely beautiful.'

In role-playing submissive scenarios, the dom is often supposedly making you unhappy – humiliated, in pain – but they know that this is really want you want; otherwise, why are you both there? As I let myself go more, leaned in to how my body was feeling and away from my conscious brain chatter, I realised my body tended to show the enthusiasm that the scenario required, even when I couldn't say it with words (and quite often I literally couldn't, because I was gagged). My regular partner Tom – Erika's husband – often says, after a couple of hours of restraining me with elaborate equipment and fucking my cunt stretched and raw with that enormous cock of his, that his favourite thing about domming me is just how much I clearly want it.

It turns out, attraction is not about your weight, the size of your boobs, how pretty your face is, your sense of enigmatic mystery, or *being cool*. I've reclaimed slutty Tigger, and the broken sofa and coffee table are well worth it.

Anthony had become inextricably linked with pain, elaborate theatrical settings and an intense sense of drama. He was also helping me process so many of the questions I had around the practices I was exploring. He was older and significantly more experienced, but he was also extremely well-read and thoughtful on the topics of domination and submission, trust and consent, and reconciling the desire for violence in sex with the horror of it in life. I had met up with him a few more times, always as a photoshoot, and at each session something new had happened and I found something strange and wonderful within myself. Max was delighted by it all. He and Anthony would comment on each other's pictures on nude photography and fetish websites, and chat online. We all knew the particular dynamic probably wouldn't work with all three of us there, but I liked that there was some communication between them. I definitely took the pain-accepting skills I was learning with Anthony out to the clubs and parties I went to with Max; I was getting braver, and I was finding it easier and easier to get into the headspace where everything felt electric and ecstatic.

Anthony told me he had a surprise for me. This was terrifying and exciting in equal measure. He had not told me how to dress, so I put on nice lingerie and a slinky but demure, grey dress, along with stockings and boots. I was feeling increasingly nervous – this was to be the first time I was seeing him solely as a submissive. Before, there had always been at least the pretext of photography, and had framed our activities. Without that, what would the narrative be?

The cab pulled up and I got out and rang the bell of his beautiful townhouse. He opened the door and said hello, briefly kissing me on the lips. He ushered me into the dining room with its big antique table, decorated with candlestands. There were maybe ten chairs around it. An incredibly beautiful girl was sitting at the table. She smiled laconically and introduced herself as Camille. She was very feline, with perfect cheekbones, huge eyes and luminous skin – I couldn't see her body, as she was wearing an oversized, soft cashmere jumper. There was a bottle of Ruinart on the table and three cut-crystal champagne flutes. I sat down opposite her as directed, leaving the seat at the head of the table for Anthony. I could feel my heart pounding, as it was clear that she knew exactly who I was and why I was there, but I had no idea what role she was to play.

I was coming to realise that one element of the theatrical role play in which Anthony was such a specialist was this sense of uncertainty. There was something delicious about the suspense. He knew what was going to happen, and I did not. When Max and I met up with others for sex dates – threesomes, foursomes – sexy and fun as they were, they were usually devoid of that *What is going to happen next?* feeling. We would have already been on a normal date in a bar, usually, and then arranged to play on a separate occasion if everyone was up for it. In some ways, the surprise meetings of normal life – flirting on a plane, or meeting someone at a dinner party and wondering what their glance meant – might have more suspense than pre-planned sex dates, and that is perhaps why I would never want to exclusively meet people through kinky apps and websites, and rule out the wonderful chance and uncertainty of day-to-day existence.

In a world where really only one thing is certain, and that is your own death, perhaps playing with the feeling of not knowing where events are going is some kind of comforting denial of mortality.

Anthony poured the drinks and we began a surreally polite conversation; very nervously in my case, leisurely in Camille's, and somehow simultaneously laidback, watchful and controlling in Anthony's. I learned that Camille was a professional model from Paris, though she lived in LA. Even though she was very sweet and friendly, I felt completely intimidated by her. After a while, Anthony said we had to go upstairs. Camille excused herself and went somewhere – it transpired she was staying with Anthony for a shoot and thus had a bedroom, though I did not know that at this point. I walked upstairs ahead of Anthony, to the sitting room we had previously shot in. He sat down in an armchair.

'Pour me a drink and kneel down in front of me.'

I poured the wine he gestured to, and knelt down in front of the chair. He lifted my chin with his finger and said quietly, 'You are very beautiful, you know,' and then slapped my face, extremely hard.

I screamed.

'Shhhh,' he said, in a way that made me know I had to be quiet. He held my chin and slapped my cheek, the same cheek, over and over.

I think there may be three mental stages when it comes to repeated pain. The first is a kind of shock or panic, a *Fuck me, this hurts, I can't do it*. The second is a sort of rational brain takeover: *I think this might actually bruise, I have work tomorrow* . . . And then, after a lot of real, hard slaps to the face, while looking up at the person doing it, there is a perfect moment of present-ness, where you know that you are just there, and the voices in your head – of pain, or anxiety about the week, or worry about what's going to happen next, or really anything at all – are silenced, and you feel perfectly surrendered to whatever will happen.

'Beauty can be usurped,' he said.

Anthony told me to take off my dress and kneel back down. I did as directed. Camille then appeared. I felt that the two of them had pre-choreographed everything, which made me feel like I was in a kind of fetish immersive theatre production. She was wearing a long, slinky black dress and looked amazing. She didn't smile.

Anthony looked at her and said, 'She's all yours.'

She walked slowly over to me, and looked down at me, still kneeling in front of Anthony. She bent down and put her face close to mine and looked me in the eyes. Then, suddenly, she hit me squarely across the jaw. I cried out; it really hurt. She looked at me, and told me to remove my earrings. I know this was a sensible concern, but she managed to say it in a way that made me very afraid. She proceeded to slap and hit my face more brutally than Anthony had, bringing tears to my eyes. After this, she stood up and walked to the adjacent sofa, and languidly sat down.

Anthony stroked my head, and then pulled off my bra. 'Stand up and take off your knickers.'

My face was stinging. I stood up in my shoes and hold-ups, and took off my knickers.

In a withering voice, Camille said, 'Fold them and put them neatly over there.'

I did so, then knelt back down. Anthony put his hand between my legs and pushed a finger into my cunt. I hadn't really noticed how turned on I was becoming because I was in a face-stinging trance. However, as soon as I felt his hand there, I realised I was already ridiculously close to coming and my cunt was dripping. Anthony noticed too.

'My, you're very wet,' he said, making me feel humiliated for being so turned on just from being slapped and forced to strip in front of a beautiful dominatrix model. He pulled me up onto his lap and hugged me. I sensed his hug as controlling or lulling me into a sense of security before something else to come, and yet I wanted to hang on to it for as long as I could.

He pushed me onto the floor and made me bend over, with my face on the ground and bottom in the air. He spanked me hard until I was tingling all over. Then, once again, he pushed his fingers into my cunt, embarrassing me on purpose by showing he knew how wet I was. Camille sat on the sofa, coolly watching.

Then he gave me to Camille. He said, 'I want you to go to her now, and obey her.' He sat back in the chair, and lit a cigar.

I crawled over to her and knelt in front of her.

'How does it make you feel if your master can just give you away like this?' she said, with no hint of a smile.

I looked at Anthony, and he didn't move or say anything. 'Ummm, I don't know. Like I should do everything you say and try to please you, and that will please him?'

'Of course. But how do you *feel*? I mean, you are kneeling naked in front of two people who can, and will, do anything they like to you.'

I could feel myself blushing, because the obvious answer was 'turned on' but that was, of course, the humiliating answer too.

After more interrogation, she asked me to bend over the sofa and spanked me hard. Then she told me to get up and pour drinks. Once I'd done that, she said I had to go to her room and bring down a pair of shoes I would find there. I did so, realising that she had sent me away because she wanted to discuss something with Anthony. Part of me thought, *Oh no, she is not having fun, she doesn't like me*. Another part of me thought, *Perhaps she wants to concoct some devious scheme with Anthony . . .*

I went to the guest room and found her vintage shoes, tiny sized with a scary heel. I brought them back with me. Camille stretched out her feet and told me to put them on her; I did.

Anthony instructed me to get a suitcase from behind the sofa. I brought out an ancient, battered leather case and placed it on the floor in front of us all. I confess I was happy, because I knew this was not the case with the canes in, and the lack of canes present was making me relieved. I opened it up. Camille told me to show her what was in it. So, one by one, I laid out gags, floggers, whips, straps, paddles, ropes and cuffs.

All of Anthony's possessions are beautiful, historic, well-worn and full of stories. The leather strap feels like it might have been present in a Victorian school. The carved mahogany handles of the floggers have been shaped by his strong grip. Worn-down places on the ropes speak to exactly where another submissive tried to struggle, her wrists or ankles fraying them. As I reverently touched each item, I had a sense of being part of a grand lineage of his submissives. I hoped I could live up to them.

Camille picked up a leather ball gag, and pulled me to my feet. She looked me in the eyes as she pushed the ball into my mouth and tightened the strap around the back of my head. Then she bent me over so that my hands were on the sofa, but I was still standing in my heels and stockings, legs spread. Then she went to town. It seemed she wanted to try every single one of Anthony's tools, almost to christen each one herself. Everything hurt, and soon it felt entirely magical. At one point I looked around and I saw that she had pulled off the top of her dress and her big, smooth, round breasts were out, sweat glistening between them – like she needed to channel a naked warrior-woman brutality to get the right force.

Finally, she gave me back to Anthony, who put me on the floor, roughly took off the gag, pressed my face into the ground and pushed his fingers into me. I felt so close to coming anyway, and I think he could tell, so he kept fingering me, and pressing my clit. I felt very exposed, with my legs spread and my forehead on the ground in a complete position of submission. I felt waves of orgasm begin to overwhelm me and started to shout out.

'What do you say?' asked Camille.

'Please . . . please,' I said.

'No, what do you say?' said Anthony.

I was all stupid with being so turned on and in a pain-trance, so I said, 'Please make me come!'

Of course they both laughed.

'Did you hear what she said? *Make* her come?' Camille said.

'Ahhh, I'm sorry. Please *let* me, please *allow* me to come.' Finally, I came fully, unable to hold back my guttural, animal noises, as they both stood up and looked at me crouched and naked, trembling and spasming on the wooden floor.

Afterwards, I was invited to sit up. They talked to each other and passed me a glass of wine, but I remained kneeling and naked while they sat in their chairs. They both lit cigarettes and I held the ashtray.

Anthony asked me to get a different case. I recognised this one. I mentally thanked him for waiting till I had had some wine and a breather. He made me lay down the case and open it, and then told me I knew what to do. I stood up and bent over the sofa, with my arms and legs totally straight and braced. Camille took out her camera – as well as being a model, she was also Anthony's photography student, it transpired.

This time was less brutal than when Anthony was trying to get a particular effect for photos, and had to go over the exact same spot multiple times. But somehow it was worse, because he could hit anywhere – inner thighs, lower back. The sound of the cane cracking is like nothing else; it is a white noise that continues after it lands, and your mind is blank with the pain.

He picked me up eventually and drew me into him. I was all sweaty and my make-up had run. All the while, Camille sat there, so composed. He stroked my hair and told me he was so pleased with me, and that I was beautiful and I was good. Then he told me to put pegs on my nipples. I did so, but in the least painful way. He shook his head, violently flicked them off, and then reattached them, making sure they pinched deeply enough to really hurt.

Then he asked if I thought Camille deserved some attention. She raised an eyebrow at him. It made me smile, thinking there was no way he was domming her in a million years.

'Do you think she deserves to lick your cunt?' Anthony asked Camille.

Camille sighed. 'I'm not sure.'

Anthony said, 'She would be so grateful.' He looked at me, and of course I nodded. Aside from the vast surge of submissive gratitude and desire to please her I had felt within the theatrical scene we had created, I also thought she was extremely hot and would have wanted to fuck her in any context.

Camille stood up. Her top was still off, but she pulled off the dress entirely and sat down in a different armchair, spreading her legs and placing her heeled feet on the floor on either side of me. She pulled off the pegs from my nipples, maybe marginally less brutally than Anthony would have.

I approached her, and gingerly stroked her slim, muscular legs, looking at her cunt. It was glistening with moisture, and I really wanted to touch it. I began to gently stroke her, and kiss her thighs, and then lick her with my tongue. She grabbed my hair, and pushed my head down. I could taste her cunt. I licked deep inside her, then pushed my fingers in, and she shouted, 'Harder!' as she pressed my face onto her clit. I fucked her harder and harder with my fingers, feeling my face getting wetter and wetter, until she was crying out and coming repeatedly.

She pulled on her dress, and immediately was composed and supercilious again. 'Thank you, Anthony,' she said, looking at him, not me.

Anthony told me to come back to him and kneel down.

Camille lit a cigarette and had a drink, and she and Anthony talked. When I tried to join in, Anthony told me to shut up. Camille asked Anthony some advice about domming two men at once. And then she said she was going to bed.

When she had gone, Anthony asked me if I liked my surprise. I said yes. He bent me over his lap and fingered me relentlessly, not stopping when I came, or cried, or shook.

Eventually, he pushed me off his lap and slapped my face hard a few times. Then it was time to go. I got dressed and we went downstairs. The cab called to say he was there, but Anthony pushed me quickly into the dining room, and forced me down over the table. He whacked my bottom with his hand on top of the cane marks, knowing it would cause the pain to rebound, and then pushed his fingers inside me for a last time, so he could feel once again the strange, immediate connection between the pain he caused me and the gushing of my cunt. Then he pulled me up, said I had been very good, and kissed me on the cheek. I left and got into the cab.

Our world does not make trust easy. Most of us have had our credit cards cloned or our phones grabbed out of our hands. We have all been let down, maybe even abandoned, by parents, friends or lovers. The institutions in which we are supposed to have faith are shown time and again to be corrupt or negligent – the government, the police force, the medical profession. We know the risks of trusting what we see online, with deep fakes lurking round every internet corner. How can we possibly trust anyone or anything in a universe like this?

I wonder, actually, if the fact that trust is such a rare commodity is what makes it feel so beautiful and precious when you find it. When we do find people we really trust, and we can be completely ourselves with them, it feels like this is what human connection is supposed to be, what existence itself is for. For me, offering my skin to a cane-wielding dom is an act of trust – but I am not sure if it's really any more so than sharing my hopes, dreams or desires with a partner or friend. Both are extremely vulnerable places to be, and to me, both are definitely worth the risk.

So much that is worthwhile involves 'trusting the process'. Artists have to believe that each line they draw is contributing to something beautiful; writers often talk about the work involved in keeping the belief, not letting the self-doubt wheedle in and stop their novel in its tracks. In recovery, addicts are exhorted to 'take it one day at a time', and *trust* that if they do, the substance-free days will become months and years. 'Practise, practise, and all is coming,' said Patthabhi Jois, the now-controversial father of Ashtanga vinyasa yoga. By this, he meant that you have to trust that if you keep showing up every day, then one day, your legs will be behind your head, however unlikely it seems at first.

I was learning to trust myself; every time some new iteration of pain or humiliation resulted in making me more aroused than ever before, this made me trust that my body and mind would always behave in this way. The more I saw Anthony, the more I trusted that while he would test my boundaries and push me further, I would enjoy it; and that in reality, I would be entirely safe.

There are so many different things that contribute to the building of trust, and they are different for everyone. For me, proof of competence and experience seems to go a long way, as does articulate, thoughtful communication. I also need to show a dom that they can trust me – that I will say if things are too much, and that I understand my body and emotions enough to do whatever we're doing.

But safety is only the very first part. Most of all, I need to trust that it will be life-changingly, cunt-gushingly, *fun*.

❧

For a long time, Anthony and I only existed for each other in the context of our theatrical roles. We did not hang out; we were not platonic friends or vanilla lovers. We were not connected on Facebook, and we did not know what the other did for a living. This, for me, made it easier to accept pain and humiliation – there was no transition phase from an ordinary role to a submissive one. In contrast, with Max it was much harder to get into the right mental state of surrender and acceptance, because our relationship also involved day-to-day life, roast chickens and board games, families, holidays – love. If Max grabbed me and bent me over a chair and spanked me, I could accept far fewer strokes, because my head would not be automatically in that submissive place – which is not to say I did not enjoy it.

This meant, though, that it was hard to ask Anthony questions. I was so curious about him and his backstory – and who was Camille? What was going on? How had he planned it all? Years later, he did tell me what had happened. I was lying naked, face down over his lap on a sofa, my head to one side, after several hours of spanking and caning. He was balancing an ashtray on my throbbing arse, reclining back into the sofa. In this position of perfect comfort for both of us, we reminisced about long-past sessions. He told me that Camille had been a house guest; they were acquaintances through photography and she was working in London for a few weeks. He had explained to her that I would be coming over as his sub, and asked if she wanted to go out, or, if that was inconvenient, he said he could reschedule me. On the contrary, she had asked if she could stay and be a part of the proceedings, as it was something she was interested in exploring. I assumed she had been an experienced – even professional – dominatrix, but this was far from the case. He admitted he had been concerned she was going too far; he had finally stopped her work on me, knowing I would be in too much of a state to notice if it was really too much. He knew she was inexperienced and might get carried away, or not read the situation correctly. It sounded like he had been on high alert, which was certainly not the vibe he had given at the time. He told me they were still in touch, and her career was going extremely well, but he did not know if she had ever gagged, flogged, spanked and come over any other willing women. I felt extremely special.

I loved the way Max and I were recording our journey down the fetish rabbit hole through the medium of photography, but it is not my first way of understanding desire. If we watch a good film, his first compliment will be for the cinematography, and mine will definitely be for the screenplay. I'm a reader; I like words. For me, no photo – or video – could be as arousing as a story well told through words alone. Max knew I loved reading classic erotica – I would revisit Georges Bataille, Henry Miller, the Marquis de Sade and Anaïs Nin in the same way people find comfort in reading Jane Austen again and again. I knew that so many of the scenarios that seeped into my imagination and out of my mouth as suggestions had probably come from books like these. I loved the discovery that my desire for pain and humiliation was as old as, well, the printing press at least. I heard about Georgian erotic chapbooks – stories printed on pamphlets and distributed discreetly through Paris and London. If you knew, you knew.

Historically, there is a fascinating connection between free thinking and writing about sex. In 1802, at the tail end of the Georgian era in England, the Society for the Suppression of Vice was founded. It meant that people could be prosecuted for immoral activity, which was defined as: 'Profanation of the Lord's Day and profane swearing; publication of blasphemous, licentious and obscene books and prints; selling by false weights and measures; keeping of disorderly public houses, brothels and gaming houses; procuring; illegal lotteries; cruelty to animals.'

Plenty of Georgians ridiculed this new law, but its real purpose was possibly to enable the prosecution of potential revolutionaries – the Crown was scared of what had just happened in France. An 'obscene' book could be one that questioned authority, as well as those that featured erotica. But by the time the much more puritan Victorian age was in full swing, they got specific, and in 1857 the Obscene Publications Act came in; the same act under which D.H. Lawrence was prosecuted in 1960, albeit with a 1959 amendment about literary merit.

In the early nineteenth century, there was an area in London called 'Booksellers' Row' in what is now Aldwych. Here, two streets were devoted to shops selling pornographic writing. William Dugdale was the area's most famous proprietor. He was a publisher, printer and seller, and despite his shops frequently being raided by the police, and him spending a lot of time in prison, he seemed undaunted. His books were sought after throughout the country, with the efficient Victorian postal service meaning they could be mailed to you next-day delivery. Along with erotica, he published subversive political tracts – again, it could be that these were what the authorities were more concerned about. The most famous example of this attitude must be the Marquis de Sade – his incarceration was ostensibly about decency, but in reality more about political subversion. In her book *The Sadeian Woman*, Angela Carter talks about how full of equality and freedom Sade's violent fantasies are, and it is that element that was truly subversive.

It is bizarre that the establishment has so often worried about people writing about their sexual proclivities. Are they afraid that once we all realise our desires are normal, we will cease to be ashamed and somehow then rise up en masse against the government? It's not dissimilar to Nixon creating the War on Drugs as a means to prosecute the free-loving, acid-tripping hippies who were so against his precious Vietnam War. Sexual freedom is considered threatening, which goes to show how ingrained sexual shame and conservatism are in society. Even if today in the West you're unlikely to be prosecuted for penning an 'obscene' novel, you may still be banned from Instagram for showing a nipple.

As I began to keep my diary of sexual and kink encounters, I learned so much more about myself, reflecting on why *this* worked and *that* I could take or leave. Writing was selective, of course – I couldn't describe every single detail. What didn't make the cut, and what loomed large in my mind, was sometimes surprising. A small detail, a look, a direction, the curtains – sometimes I felt more like committing that to my diary than the more explicit elements. And what I loved most was that everything that had been so arousing at the time became so again the next day when I had to relive it in mental technicolour in order to transcribe it. Sometimes I would write only a paragraph a day, ensuring I spent a week almost torturing myself with heady memories. I thought about Henry Miller and Anaïs Nin writing their porn-for-cash stories in wartime New York; although transactional, and a bit of a joke, did this lead to their exploring their sexuality in real life, and their subsequent revered documentation of it? Does writing about sex make you more interested in it, or would you only be writing about it if you were already thoughtful about the topic?

Gradually, shyly, I began occasionally to share the diaries with the people they involved, too. The response was fascinating. Sometimes, people would tell me what had been going on in their own heads at the moments I was describing. Sometimes, they were surprised – 'I had no idea the pegs were hurting your nipples that much!' Occasionally, they were a bit hurt by omission – 'I can't believe you missed out the bit where I made you lie in your own piss! That was my favourite!' They might laugh at the odd erroneous detail – 'I would never have given you Prosecco', 'You were so *not* on time'. Most often of all, they tell me they have had a wank, reliving the events through my words.

Over the years, the writing has become a key part of my sex life. I gleefully torment one friend I logistically can't see very often by sending him highly anonymised versions of stories featuring others. One West Coast dom friend occasionally demands a story of me, presumably when at a loose end, and after enjoying it, loves to tell me what a completely unbelievably filthy slut I am. This usually leads to time zone-incompatible phone sex.

As I started feeling more confident about sharing my escapades in written form with the partners involved, the sex and play with them definitely got better. I realised that on paper, I could be more open about what worked for me, and share my feelings about what we did, blow by blow. Imagine if all lovers came with a manual like that. And, as I tended to be extremely effusive about my enjoyment, I think there was no small element of pride for those doms who saw themselves reflected in my helplessly turned-on submissive eyes. Of course, I never shared any true or identifying features of one person with another, or any intimate or personal knowledge. The diaries were my version of our photography – a suggestive snapshot, with faces tantalisingly hidden.

Body

A sad fact of the Western world today – and for the last few hundred years – is that we seem to have decided to guillotine our minds from our bodies, slicing away our physical selves like a Philip Pullman daemon in Svalbard. When Descartes uttered his horrible phrase, 'I think therefore I am,' it was a tragic day, relegating every part of human experience outside the conscious mind as somehow irrelevant to existence itself. This supposedly 'enlightened' thinking suggested that any group that represented the physical more than the intellectual – like women, with their propensity to bleed every month and give birth to babies, or indigenous peoples who have a 'primitive' physical and instinctive understanding of nature – could be considered inferior and therefore be subjugated. This line of thinking also glorified certain senses over others, celebrating what we can see and hear, while undervaluing touch, taste and smell. Visual art, literature and music can be studied at the world's most prestigious universities – but not dance, perfumery or cooking. Older Eastern traditions revered the body. The ancient Greeks celebrated sensory experience. Medieval writing is filled with bones, blood, gore, decay and sex. The Georgians had a very physical attitude to sex before Victorian morality stamped it out. By contrast, modern Western medicine treats the body as a piece of machinery we all own, one that can hopefully be fixed by a skilled mechanic, rather than as a fundamental and equal part of ourselves. Only recently have Western science and culture begun to understand the connection between what we think in our minds and what we feel in our bodies; a concept that other traditions, like Chinese medicine, have long held as central tenets. Recent bestselling books like *The Body Keeps the Score* by Bessel van der Kolk, where we learn how emotional trauma is written on our bodies, *Food for Life* by Tim Spector, where we see how interconnected the gut is with the brain, or *Breath* by James Nestor, which shows the miraculous changes we can make to our brains simply by how we breathe, are thankfully teaching us all that we are much more than an intelligent computer encased in a physical shell.

Personally, I'm convinced that to live a life without paying attention to all our senses and how we can experience the world through them is not just sad, but also likely to result in sickness, and I am sure that it is one reason why anxiety, depression and other mental health conditions are so rife.

Athletes, dancers and yogis all report that you can learn something in your conscious mind, but it is only when you start to understand it in your body that it begins to work. If you have ever been to a yoga class, you're likely to have heard every yoga teacher's favourite instruction: 'Knit your ribs together!' And, you've probably thought, as I did the first time I heard it, *What the hell does that mean? How do I knit my ribs together? What?* But after a while, and perhaps with a teacher physically adjusting you to show you on your body, you will begin to grow the muscles around your rib cage, and you will work out how to engage them to support your torso and straighten your spine. But this process isn't conscious; it is happening at a deep, physical level.

We all have physical instincts, but we don't always listen to them. A surfer once told me she sometimes gets in the ocean and can feel that something is wrong. The water feels wrong on her skin, but she can't say why; she can't consciously see a bad current or weather pattern. But she has learned to listen, because every time she's had that feeling, she has been proved right. She described this intuition physically; it was a deep gut feeling, not a thought in her mind.

It's no accident that techniques for becoming more present, and not living in the future or past via chatter in our brains, often involve paying attention to our bodies: noticing the breath, placing a hand on the rising stomach, or feeling the air move on the skin under the nose. The body scan – where you send your attention to each body part one by one – is one of the most used sleep relaxation techniques. I think it works not because it's distracting you from your conscious thoughts, but because it is reminding you on a physical level that your mind is not all you are. A thought is just a thought; it isn't you.

The same thing happens in sex and kink. As I became more confident that I understood what I was doing, that I could consciously articulate and communicate what I wanted and understand what others were saying to me, the words began to give way to a deeper and more physical understanding. Sometimes it is hard to describe in words what is happening. We can feel it in our bodies, using all our senses, and when our bodies commune with others, something bigger, something more ancient and more human, occurs.

❧

As usual, I was having palpitations of nervous anxiety, if not outright terror, on the way to Anthony's; as usual, I had no idea what to expect. It was 11.30 a.m. on a bright, sunny spring day. I was wearing my slouchy blue dress with nothing on underneath, just hold-ups and my little black Acne boots. I could have been going to brunch.

Anthony opened the door, kissed me hello, then turned me around against the hall wall, pressing my face into it as he pushed his fingers up into my cunt – which was completely wet from all the nervous 'what ifs?' that had been going around my head on the way over. He fingered me loudly so I could hear how wet I was, then pulled me round to face him.

'Go downstairs and put your coat and dress on the peg by the downstairs bathroom.'

Of course, I did this without questioning him, even though I wondered why he wanted me to put them there, and not on the pegs in the hall like usual – what was going to happen in the basement?

I came back upstairs in just my hold-ups and shoes, and found Anthony in the kitchen, leaning against the counter. He told me to make him a cup of coffee, somehow imbuing this mundane task with gravitas and menace. He dictated each step of the complex, ritualistic procedure, and sighed witheringly when I couldn't see the milk at first. Then, when I accidentally got the sugar spoon wet, he bent me over the counter and spanked me extremely hard.

We went upstairs, and I knelt in front of him on the floor as he sat on the sofa; I knew enough by then never to sit in his chairs. He slapped my face hard a few times, until my eyes were stinging. I wondered how I could cope with a whole day at his hands; I knew that I couldn't relax, because as soon as I did a new barrage of pain would come raining down somewhere. But I reminded myself that I had no choice in the matter at all; there is no point worrying about something you can't do anything about. However serene I can make my mind, however, my body does not agree. It had been a trembling, nervy, hypersensitive and hyper-aroused wreck from the moment I walked in the door.

Anthony said that he had a model coming over for a shoot. He went to collect her from the station, telling me to put my dress on and that I would make them coffee when she arrived. Of course, I wondered what he would tell her about who I was, but naturally I did not ask. She arrived, and they sat in the sitting room and discussed their shoot as I brought coffee. She was called Alanna, and had a beautiful aquiline face, cropped bright red hair and tattoos all over. She seemed composed but reserved, so I didn't really understand why she was modelling or what sort of world she was in. Anthony shoots porn stars and all manner of kinky people, but also plenty of fashion models and pretty 'normal' people too. As she went to get ready, Anthony told me to choose a book from his shelves, then take the suitcase – the very sight of which scared me – from behind the sofa and go downstairs. There, I was to wait in the spare room in the basement, once again taking off my dress and leaving it on the peg.

I went down the stone steps to the basement. There was a small room, sparsely furnished, with what I thought of as a Victorian hospital-style bedstead – a white painted steel bar frame. After a few minutes, Anthony came down. He opened the suitcase and pulled out cuffs, a collar and a lead. It was the first time I had seen these. I wondered what the significance was, if any; I wasn't sure, but as most things are quite ritualistic and non-accidental with him, it all felt very proprietorial. He put my hands into the cuffs, clipping them together behind my back, then knelt me down at the foot of the bed, looping the lead around the foot of the bedpost. He pushed me onto my face and spanked me, then fingered me hard till I was gasping. Then he stood up and opened my book – I had selected *The Beautiful and the Damned* – placing it in front of me on the bed. With a smile, he said, 'I'm sure you can turn the pages with your nose.' Then he closed the door behind him and went upstairs.

I had no way of knowing how long he would be, but this did not really concern me. Although I couldn't move very much at all, I was not uncomfortable. Anthony had kindly put a soft blanket under my knees. I found that I could turn the pages of the book with my tongue and nose, and I could press it open with my head. However, the lives of F. Scott Fitzgerald's characters paled in contrast to the stories in my own head. I was in a happy part-fantasy, part-reality world – the situation was so similar to those

I had previously imagined or read about. I was thinking of O chained at the foot of the bed in the castle in *The Story of O*, only being taken out to have obscene acts of sex and violence performed upon her by her lover and the other men. My only frustration was that I couldn't reach to touch myself and make myself come. I was even nervous about rubbing myself on the eiderdown, as I knew I was bleeding and feared I'd make a big mess. I have little shame about period blood; like most bodily fluids, it feels natural, and, like sweat, cum or piss, it only ever smells bad later on when bacteria develops, not when it's leaving your body. I had asked Anthony if he minded in advance, out of politeness and an awareness that he should have control over all aspects of my body. He did not mind, but I knew dirtying an antique quilt would be a good excuse for extra pain.

After some time, I have no idea how long, Anthony came back down. He said I looked nice, and pulled me over the bed, spanking me a little and pushing his fingers into my wet cunt. He could see he would make me come in a second, so he stopped, pushed me back onto my knees and closed the door, leaving to continue the shoot. More time elapsed. I was perfectly happy; my hands were going a little bit cold and numb behind my back, and I had pins and needles in my legs, but I could wriggle enough to make it fine. I had the odd itch and hair in my mouth, but mostly I was too preoccupied with enjoying being so entirely at Anthony's mercy in this new way.

Eventually he came down again and untied me, and told me Alanna would like to shoot with me. He took off my cuffs and collar, and told me to go up to his bedroom on the top floor, warning me not to bleed all over his white sheets. I realised I had never been in his bedroom before, though I had seen pictures he had shot in there. I went upstairs. Alanna was lying naked in the bed; she had a really beautiful body, and the light was falling across her stomach and breasts. I felt a bit uncomfortable, as I still didn't really know what she would be up for, and whether Anthony basically wanted us to have sex while he watched, or if it was simply a very artistic photoshoot. Even in this scenario, Alanna was very reserved and I couldn't really tell. Much as I *love* the uncertainty and sense of not knowing what will happen to me, and would usually be delighted to be told to perform depraved sexual acts on someone I'd just met in front of the camera, you just can't assume. I didn't want to abdicate all responsibility for her to Anthony and think, *Oh, he must have ensured she's fine with this.* Although I knew he would have, 'assuming' is the enemy of consent.

Anthony arranged us in the bed, placing our hands on each other and moving us into very intimate positions. She was extremely relaxed, but she also didn't seem enthusiastic about making it more 'real'. He did keep checking that she was comfortable with everything. Amusingly, at one point he said, 'Oh, and Sonnet, you must tell me if *you're* uncomfortable with anything too,' in a voice dripping with sarcasm as he stroked a finger down my back. He made us kiss, but I was too unsure of her to really kiss her, so it was all playacting. I wish I had, as she was beautiful, but I really wasn't feeling enough enthusiastic positive consent.

The light faded, so we stopped shooting. Anthony made coffees and sat in a chair as we both sat naked in his bed, talking about this and that. I gleaned that Alanna had recently become a full-time professional model after a few years of doing amateur and erotic modelling via the websites I was also on, thanks to Max. I think she had just moved to London from Scandinavia. She didn't reveal if she was into BDSM in her personal life or if it was purely for modelling. She was beautifully comfortable in her own body, and happy sitting and chatting totally naked with two people she'd just met – she didn't seem in a rush to get dressed and leave. It was freezing upstairs, so we relocated to the sitting room. She sat on the sofa and Anthony sat on the armchair, gesturing for me to kneel at his feet. I of course obeyed.

He turned to Alanna and said, 'As you can see, Sonnet is submissive. Are you more comfortable with domination or submission?'

She said she didn't fall easily into either category. Again, I noticed how amazingly reserved she was, and sighed inwardly, wishing I could do 'cool and enigmatic', instead of 'massively oversharing, talking too much, and generally acting like a Labrador puppy'.

'Have you ever been caned, Alanna?' he asked.

She said no. He said she must have seen the marks in his pictures, and she said she had, and she was extremely curious about it, but not on her own body.

'Would you like to see Sonnet being caned?'

She said she would be extremely intrigued to see this. Anthony made me bend over the sofa that Alanna was sitting on, and gave me about six hard strokes. I managed to say thank you after each one, and I tried not to move and cry, but it was so hard. I didn't think I was getting any better at it, despite Anthony telling me I was; I think he just said it to make me feel proud and want to prove it more, like a teacher giving their student encouragement.

What would 'getting better at it' mean, anyway? Trying to stay still, or at least coming back to the position (arse up, back arched) if I had recoiled or moved in shock: that is what I associated with progress and what I tried so hard to do, always seeking praise. Other things happened with practice, too: I noticed that I could recover more quickly. My heart rate seemed to return to normal sooner, and I could speak again immediately; in some ways, my nervous system must have been getting more used to it. After a while, I noticed my bruises healed more quickly too. Our bodies are so extremely adaptable. But in the moment, the pain never lessened, and my excited fear about it never changed.

I was really violently shaking at the end, and Anthony gave me a hug. In retrospect, as it was about 4 p.m. and I had only eaten breakfast, I was probably extra shaky from hunger, and from having been quite cold for a while.

Anthony seemed to notice this – or perhaps it was coincidence – and suggested we go for a late lunch at the pub. Alanna said she would go home. As she was getting her things, Anthony pushed his fingers into my cunt, no doubt to see if the caning had had its usual effect. Which it had, of course.

In the pub, Anthony and I became normal, equal people, our roles relaxed. We talked about what we had been doing, and why we liked it. And then we chatted more generally. I liked getting to know his real-life personality a little bit, and telling him more about me and Max and our lives. I was beginning to find that being friends with someone did not mean I couldn't then accept them as a dom and submit to them; previously I had held the opposite to be true, as if not knowing more about them kept our dom/sub relationship sacred and intact. I was learning, though, that with some people, the growing relationship actually built even more trust, and we could travel to even more extreme places as a result.

I felt revived from lunch, happy to have got to know Anthony slightly better, and excited that we still had lots more time. I was feeling less nervy and more relaxed. This turned out to be a grave error.

Upon returning to Anthony's, he told me to hang up my dress downstairs and bring up the suitcase. He put my collar, cuffs and lead back on, and pulled me onto my hands and knees. He whipped me all over with the jellyfish – a beaded flogger – until every inch of my skin was stinging and tears were running down my cheeks. The next couple of hours was spent with Anthony beating me with various implements and his hands, occasionally asking me to make him drinks, and pulling me close to him, kissing me and lightly stroking me all over in a way that was complete torment, ticklish, and arousing. This, interchanged with the spanking and flogging, meant everything was tingling. If he touched me within about six inches of my cunt, I would violently spasm. He said languorously,

'I can play your body like a musical instrument.' This was true – if musicians achieve their melodies by subjecting their violins to a torturous mixture of pain and pleasure until they are shaking and groaning . . .

Anthony asked if I had watched the Lars von Trier film *Nymphomaniac*. I hadn't, and really wanted to. He opened an antique cupboard to reveal a TV. I chuckled inwardly to see that he was in fact a normal person who watched TV, and not entirely living in my gothic historical fantasy land. He sat down on the sofa and pulled me over his lap on my front, my hands still cuffed together behind me. He pulled the lead from my collar through my legs, so it was on my clit, then up round my bottom, where he held on to it tightly, pulling it and yanking it every so often. It was a strange and unusual way to watch a film, but I couldn't have imagined us simply sitting down next to each other, like an 'ordinary' couple having a cosy night in.

The film, unsurprisingly, features constant sex and nudity. Anthony would keep pushing his fingers into my cunt to see how that was making me feel.

In part two of *Nymphomaniac*, the eponymous nymphomaniac starts seeing a merciless sadist. Anthony said I was going to suffer exactly what she does. First, we would watch the scene, then we would pause the film and act it out. In the first example, Charlotte Gainsbourg's character is beaten so, so hard. I could barely watch, feeling terrified of how this would play out with me. Anthony paused the film. He unclipped my hands and tied them in front of me, then roughly pulled me to stand. He bent me over the sofa, my bottom raised high into the air.

In homage to the tense theatrical build-up in the film, he circled around me, creaking the leather strap menacingly. Finally, he took a huge swing and brought the strap down, harder than he had ever hit me before. I was so surprised by quite how hard it was, I screamed dementedly. He calmly walked over to the other side of the room while I composed myself. When I had stopped writhing around, he came back and gave me two more incredibly hard thrashes. And again, he paused and waited till I was still. I was trying hard to be composed, but I was trembling so much. He gave me another three strokes, then released me. He sat down on the sofa and lay me over his lap, then restarted the movie.

Soon, there was another scene with the sadist. In this one, the sadist gives the nymphomaniac a Roman thrashing, which is forty lashes with a knotted rope whip. Her bottom and legs are completely lacerated and the skin torn, with bleeding flesh exposed. Anthony pulled out the jellyfish – with its long tendrils and little knotted bits, it was a good approximation. Although I was still in a lot of pain from the leather strap, I thought this could not possibly be worse. I was wrong. Like the film's sadist, he swooshed the whip down from a great height. It was almost beyond pain. The force was incredible. It felt so abandoned, like he had finally unleased something he had been holding back. The strokes felt almost frenzied, Bacchic, so different from the calm, menacing control he'd displayed in the past. I realised I was no longer simply weeping, with tears seeping down my cheeks like normal, but actually properly crying, with wracking sobs and snot. He could see this and did not stop; despite the pain and how much I wished he would stop, I completely loved that he didn't.

When he finally stopped, I stumbled up, sobbing and shaking and sniffing, gulping for air. He pulled me in and hugged me, stroking my hair till I calmed down. I apologised for losing count of the strokes and said thank you. I had a huge rush of endorphins and adrenaline, and I felt like crying again. It was very strange, and cathartic, and painful. I felt a new, powerful surge of devotion to Anthony.

Something shifted in this session. Anthony somehow knew I was ready for something much more physically intense than we'd explored previously. Part of it was our relationship and connection deepening over the couple of years we had been seeing each other, with my trust in him, and thus my ability to surrender to him, becoming almost absolute. And from his point of view, he knew he could read my body and all its signals, enabling him to understand what it was doing for me and what I could take. But I think it was also part of a wider shift; after so much thinking and exploring and discovering, through talking, learning, reading, writing and photography, somehow I had come through this world of the mind, and was beginning to understand in my body.

At the beginning of my cycle, everything is liquid. As the deep red blood drips out of my womb, bathing my cunt, my eyes fill with water at the slightest thing – the light through the trees, an opened flower, a kind word, an angry one. My fascia seems to become liquid too – my limbs float. They are not strong, but so flexible, so malleable, they could easily be pulled into any position. I am hot, and the blood is close to my skin everywhere, but more than anywhere else, I feel it throb and pulsate in my cunt. Cycling becomes an exquisite torture; wearing jeans puts me on the brink of orgasm. A breeze between my legs can make my whole body tremble. To fuck now is pure physicality. Every cell is groaning, everything is extra sensitive. I feel everything more in my body. Pain is so much more extreme, and a finger down an inner thigh seems to rearrange the chemistry of my cells. At this time, I don't really think and fantasise and imagine; I am fully in my body and can only focus on its sensations. Some men don't like fucking women when they bleed – and no shame to anyone for their likes or dislikes, even if I'm inclined to think it's unfair that semen is seen as so much more of an acceptable fluid to be bathed in than period blood. But I find that those who do like it often delight in how responsive my body is, like an instrument under their command. And for me, an orgasm is going to relieve cramps better than any amount of ibuprofen.

The few days between my period and ovulation are strong days; they are days for getting things done and making plans. As my blood recedes from the surface of my skin, I feel calmer. My desire becomes more cerebral again; I imagine scenarios and tell them to people. I sext a lot, needing ideas and images to make me come, not just touch alone. I'm also anticipatory, like a child before

Christmas, as I have had enough cycles to know what is coming.

Oh, happy Ovulation Day! There is one glorious day every month that is better than any drug. I feel euphoric, I feel bathed in light, I feel like I have infinite energy and my body could do anything I ask of it. There are so many hot people everywhere, and they all seem to talk to me. I bounce around, essentially screaming 'I'm alive!' all day. I'm so horny, but now it's all outward facing – it's all about other people, interaction, what we might do together, not my own body. Max eyes me warily; I'm as likely to hold an impromptu house party as I am to decide to get on a plane to meet a shibari expert in Stockholm. But it is my absolute favourite time to play; I feel so full of energy and love for the world that I just want to give – my body, my brain, my soul – to one person, to a room of people . . . To be alone on this day would be a huge waste. This is a day where all human connection seems electric and beautiful. I am not scared of anything, and there is nothing anyone could suggest that I wouldn't want to try. Yes, it's a day when things may get out of hand, because the idea of pulling back just seems so unnecessary in a universe this amazing. I can usually figure out when this day will come, and I love planning the mischief that my ovulation self will take to the next level.

Then, sadly, the ovulation high recedes, and pernicious progesterone begins to course through me. I find it hard not to think of progesterone as the patriarchal punishment hormone – it's there to get you ready for pregnancy, and if you are wantonly discarding the egg, it tells you to get back in your box and remember your role in society is only to breed. It's the least fun time, a week of feeling, you know, *fine*, but not strong, bendy or energetic. I sleep badly and feel tired and headachey. Until, that is, we come to what I now call, thanks to my niece's favourite picture book, My Big Shouting Day.

My Big Shouting Day is the opposite to Ovulation Day. Everything that can go wrong, will. All human interaction is fraught with tension and aggravation. Everyone is annoying. My body can't do anything; I crash into curbs on my bike and constantly drop my possessions. I worry about pointless things and feel it in my stomach. My body reacts badly to everything – I'm hungover immediately after drinking a glass of wine, anxious and wired after a cup of coffee. I look disgusting all over, I think, and don't want anyone to see me naked.

There is only one known cure for My Big Shouting Day malaise. As I crash around the kitchen, swearing at the cupboard everything fell out of and the knife that cut my finger and the glass that threw itself on the floor, Max will come in and take the implements out of my hands, and lead me, still griping, into the bedroom, where he will ignore my grumpy protests of having a hundred annoying things to do, strip me and throw me face down on the bed. For the first couple of minutes, my progesterone-flooded brain refuses to let me have any pleasure, my thoughts still swirl around, but as he continues, my attention finally begins to submit. Somehow, the tight grasp the hormone seems to have around me loosens, as I send my focus out of my brain and down and in. No light strokes will work today; I need to be pounded, hard, to get out of my own head. It takes me longer to come – I can get there, but not quite, again and again. But Max is persistent, and when it finally arrives, a Big Shouting Orgasm might be the best kind of all . . .

Of course, the invention of the pill started a trajectory of liberation that makes possible for me to live as I do, and it is a crucial, life-saving medicine for some women with endometriosis and many other conditions. But every time I tried it, I found I missed my own hormones too much. The extremes of desire and emotion I feel at different times, and the different types of sex I can have, were too great a loss. If you have to use condoms anyway (and we do – stay safe, kids!), I think I can live without extra pregnancy protection. Max and I can fuck condomless, as we are careful, we test, and I know he will pull out and come on my face. I fantasise, though, about being tied to a bed in a dark room at the edge of a party, and countless men coming in and one by one fucking me and filling me up with their cum. It's dark and they can barely see me; I'm just one increasingly full hole. They can feel the other cum inside me as they fuck me, and how slutty that is turns them on. They can feel my cunt clench around them as I get excited at the thought of the next load I will take.

Maybe I'll go on the pill for a couple of weeks, and make it happen.

❧

Max and I thought we had spent more time alone together in the four months from the start of the pandemic than we had in the previous eleven years. He was furloughed, and I was crazily busy, but in a pretty constant state of arousal, knowing that at any point of the day, he could come up behind me in the makeshift office I had built in an alcove, pull off my top and push me to my knees. The streets were quiet, the weather was warm, and often our interpretation of the decreed hour's permitted outside exercise was a dusk walk, with me in only a slip dress that could be lifted up to show my cunt to the sky.

We had got to know our downstairs neighbour Amani well. We shared a garden, and in the warm weather she would bring out pots of hot, fragrant tea with thick gold-top milk, or a bowl of strained yoghurt with about twenty cloves of raw garlic chopped into it and some pitta, as we tried to get Zoom to work outside. Lockdown was hard for her. She lived in the basement studio alone while she studied for a PhD. Her family were on the other side of the world. She was loud and opinionated and ridiculously clever; she had big dark eyes, full lips, and thick black hair. We had taken to topless sunbathing in the garden – much to Max's delight – so I knew she had big, round, soft breasts.

The weather had turned, Amani had caught the dreaded virus, and she had been completely isolated in her tiny flat for a couple of weeks. Her texts sounded sad, even though she was now better. I decided it would be ludicrous not to invite her up the stairs for dinner one night, whatever the rules might currently say.

I had been cooking a lot. The messier, the stickier, the more elaborate, the better. I spent hours dipping my hands in melted butter to make kubaneh bread, or stretching and thwacking biangbiang noodles. Max had joined the sourdough craze, and I loved the smell of

Charlemagne-the-starter getting riper and more alive every day. But it was exciting to have someone else to cook for after all this time. I spent the afternoon in the kitchen, grinding spices in the pestle and mortar, massaging them into chunks of fish, licking my fingers and noticing how a tiny pinch of something could suddenly change everything, as I played with newly discovered ingredients like dried limes and black cardamom. I made caramel for homemade toffee crisps, and loved the sharp pain of dipping a finger into bubbling sugar; the adrenaline rush of a tiny burn and the gleeful knowledge that *you're not supposed to do that*. I could easily spend eight hours in the kitchen, seeing every drop of fat or toss of a pan as a metaphor for other messy, sticky, physical activities . . .

Amani came upstairs. I lit all the candles and made the table beautiful. She helped me put the finishing touches to the dishes, and we spread them out and gorged ourselves on a feast. We talked about how strange it was that something as fundamentally ordinary as cooking for your friends in your home had become shadowy and transgressive because of the Covid rules – but we could also admit, just between us, that this did make it rather fun. It reminded me of how humanity, with a lot of thanks to religion, turned nudity from 'natural' to illicit and sexual – and how exciting this then makes the reveal of a naked body. Much as I get how naturists want to feel free from this manufactured idea, the thought of nakedness becoming everyday and ordinary, devoid of erotic feeling, exhibitionism, shame or humiliation, would, to me, be a great loss. It's at our peril that we don't admit that breaking rules feels good – and isn't part of growing up discovering those rules you can break in order to enjoy deliciously rebellious feeling, without hurting anyone else, or going to prison.

After dinner, we moved to the sofas.

'Ohhhh, I know, let's play *Chronology*!' I screeched, hyperactive from the toffee crisps, and from the much-missed evening socialising, which was filling me with intoxicating extrovert endorphins. 'It's this really exciting game where you have to put little-known events from history in chronological order. Amani, you'll be annoyingly good at it!'

Max rolled his eyes as if to say, *Way to geekify a potentially interesting situation, there, Sonnet.*

I raised my eyebrows – what else did he think could happen?

Then Amani said, 'Well, what about strip *Chronology*?'

Max suddenly looked a lot more enthusiastic.

We all knelt on the rug around the coffee table, and I dealt the cards. A couple of rounds went by with no one getting a question wrong. Then, Amani failed to guess that the tuning fork was invented in 1711. Without hesitation, she pulled off her top. She was wearing a silky bra, which I immediately wanted to stroke. Distracted, and suddenly not quite so interested in the game, I was way out on my next question too. Unfortunately, I was only wearing one item of clothing – a dress – because I had basically given up with underwear in lockdown, liking to feel always accessible to Max, and because I was very lazy about laundry. I took off the dress and knelt back down to read out the next question.

'I think this means you lost, Sonnet,' said Max.

'I'm not sure,' said Amani, inching closer to me.

This felt like a definite invitation. I turned my head to hers and kissed her, slightly shyly . . . was this definitely what she wanted? Max and I had often wondered with her; she was so tactile and friendly with us, and pretty up front about her energetic pre-Covid sex life, but there is always the risk of wishful thinking. But she kissed me back harder and began to stroke my exposed breasts.

'Ohhhh, girls are *soft*,' she said.

Max moved round behind her and unclipped her bra. She wriggled her arms out of it and I moved my lips down to her big, dark nipples, while Max started kissing her mouth. Soon, we had pulled off her trousers and knickers. Max was still fully clothed. As much as the idea of girls 'performing' as lesbians for the male gaze is ridiculous and depressing, there is something wonderful about being watched as you genuinely enjoy yourselves. In this case, being watched was certainly more exhibitionist than humiliating. As I moved my head between her legs and began to taste how wet she was getting, she made loud, deep, throaty groans, which was somehow so on brand for her it made me chuckle. We were always making fun of the way her general existence seemed to be at a volume many decibels higher than everyone else's – her speaker always on full blast, treating our whole street to politics and economics podcasts. I was delighted to see this volume applied to sex, too. As we rolled around, she kept up an excellent commentary of compliments and affirmations, interspersed with shudders and laughter as we knocked over a carafe or banged into a chair leg.

She decided Max needed some attention. He stood up and we pulled down his trousers. He took out his cock, which was tantalisingly hard.

'Oh my god, your cock is amazing,' Amani squealed in delight, and I felt bizarrely proud.

We knelt in front of him, licking his cock, our tongues touching around it. I could still taste some of the strong spices and garlic from dinner on Amani's tongue and my own, and the flavours gradually salinated with the tiny drops of Max's cum.

Eventually, we decided we should move to the bedroom.

'Sonnet, what do you like? What shall I do?' said Amani in her curious, questioning, direct way.

I thought for a second. 'Oh, I know!' I knelt down and wriggled under the bed, throwing out various boxes of ropes, latex and sex toys, trying to find what I wanted.

'Jesus, guys, you have a full-on dungeon under there!' said Amani, slightly wide-eyed.

Finally, I found what I was looking for. A strap-on, consisting of a stylish denim harness and a big, blue dildo. I thought she would look great in it.

Max and I helped her into it, and she admired herself in the mirror, stroking her blue cock thoughtfully, the harness hugging her small waist. She was so curvy, with such a stereotypically 'female' shape, that seeing her with a big cock was particularly lovely.

'Sonnet, on all fours,' said Max.

I climbed onto the bed. He helped Amani up behind me, and I looked over my shoulder to see him handing her some lube. She rubbed it on the dildo almost reverently. Then she took hold of my hips and thrust it into my waiting cunt. The angle was weird and it's a pretty long dildo, so I involuntarily gasped and winced as it hit my cervix.

'Oh, I'm sorry, I'm sorry. Hang on – wait. What if I kneel up like this – how's this? Or what about *this*? God, men have strong legs, don't they? This is a workout!' Her chatter was making me laugh, but she'd found an angle that was hitting the right spots and was still slightly painful in the best way, making me feel present, silencing my thoughts of, *Well, this is an unexpected and fun turn of events*, and blurring everything into pure physical sensation. Max climbed onto the bed in front of me and lifted my head up to his cock. I couldn't see it, but I felt them lock eyes above me, as they started fucking my mouth and my cunt together, faster and faster.

I was pretty delirious by the time they pulled out of me, and we all lay down. Amani was sweating; I wanted to lick the beads of salty liquid from between her breasts.

'Fuck me,' she said. 'I think I'm out of shape.'

I vehemently disagreed with that statement.

We had some water, and she analysed at length the peculiarities of her first time fucking a girl with a rubber strap-on, applying to the topic the kind of academic rigour that no doubt so impressed her economics supervisors. I decided it was only a truly scientific approach if she understood it from the other side as well.

Disentangling her from the harness and getting me into it turned us into one big, hysterical, multi-limbed hydra. Finally, I got to admire my own blue cock. I was never going to reach the strange, intense and immersive places I get to as a submissive, but this scenario was so funny and joyful, and such a break from the horror the whole world was experiencing, that I felt truly elated as I climbed on top of her. I thought her thighs probably needed a break, and I wanted to look at her face and her tits as I fucked her, so we rolled her onto her back and Max spread her cunt open with his hands, rubbing her clit as I gently pushed my cock into her. She gasped like I had – it really was a long dildo. I tried to move slowly, moving my hips in circles. It was pretty hard to control, being made of rubber, and I briefly fantasised to myself about having an actual penis, with blood pumping through it, making it rock hard . . .

She closed her eyes and I could feel her begin to clench and spasm beneath me, as Max alternately rubbed her clit and her nipples. I thrust my dildo cock into her faster and faster. As she began to come, she could have woken the whole borough with her screams as we tipped her over the edge.

As it got late and we got tired, we all lay in bed together, lazily chatting. I remembered we had some pistachio ice cream, and retrieved it from the kitchen. We sat up in bed, passing the tub around and giggling about the evening, the ice cream dripping onto our warm limbs as we passed the spoon back and forth. Eventually, Amani suggested she go back downstairs. That seemed cold and lonely for her, so we said she was more than welcome to sleep with us.

I woke up early the next morning, as a shaft of light fell through the curtains onto a pile of intertwined limbs. Max and Amani looked incredibly peaceful. I could already feel the physical resettling, the feeling from deep within that everything is going to be OK, that humanity is basically good if you see it up close and naked, rather than on the news or social media. It's like a big, soothing exhale, which I so often get the day after a fun, sexy encounter. I gently extracted my dead arm from under Amani's tousled head, and tiptoed to the kitchen, chuckling about the piles of bondage equipment we seemed to have left strewn around. I ground coffee beans and boiled the kettle, then slowly spiralled the water over the coffee and watched it bloom. Touch, sight, smell, taste: hand-drip is the most sensory way to make coffee. You can only do it slowly, and you're forced to notice every detail. I remembered I had *pains au chocolat* in the freezer, so I turned on the oven. I didn't want to wake Max and Amani, so I sat on the kitchen counter, looking out of the window at the birds. They seemed so much louder and active during lockdown – happier without the traffic. I wondered how many other new couplings, throuplings and beyond were happening within the households and buildings I could see. It was nice, I thought, to appreciate the people right in front of you.

I brought the coffee and pastries back into the bedroom. Max and Amani were sitting up, chatting about what a dickhead Matt Hancock is. I put the tray in the middle of the bed and sat crossed-legged at the bottom. I dropped melted chocolate on the sheets, and Amani spilled her coffee; Max said the sheets were in a worse state than the Turin Shroud at this point.

People are concerned that sex changes things between people. I think it does, but for the better. We were closer to Amani after that night, but it didn't make anything awkward. It never happened again, and Max and I never told anyone about it; I'm not sure if she did. We sat chatting in the garden as we had before. Occasionally, if no one else was around, we would reference the night we'd shared, giggling. She seemed, like us, to treat it as a fun activity with friends, not some big drama. When the world reopened, she moved abroad, but occasionally she comes to flat-sit for us when we're travelling and she wants to be in London. We tell her she knows where the strap-on lives, should she need it.

As a teenager, I was told that empowered and sexy women like fucking cowgirl style. This, according to nineties women's mags and TV, was how you got orgasms from penetrative sex, the idea being that you were in control of the rhythm, and your clit was in easy reach for both you and your partner.

The second man I ever fucked was an eighteen-year-old captain of a visiting school rugby team, who had been in the pub celebrating eviscerating my poor comprehensive on the pitch and who, in the grand tradition of horny teenagers, needed little invitation back to my house while my parents were out. I was keen to show off all my moves, so with a confidence built on sambuca shots, I straddled him and went full bucking bronco. He really seemed to enjoy it, which boosted my ego. When he came, he said he had never come before from a girl being on top, and it was fucking amazing. Of course, I was full of pride and felt like a wanton sex goddess, immediately mentally styling myself as Samantha in *Sex and the City* or Kathryn in *Cruel Intentions*. It did not occur to me to think about whether this had been in any way pleasurable for me – beyond the fact that it made me happy to make someone else happy. Incidentally, it turned out I was only the second person he had slept with, too, so his comment was hardly the grand sexual BAFTA award I'd imagined.

For a long time, I had a strange double-think around cowgirl. On the one hand, I thought it was what I was supposed to like and get pleasure from, but didn't, and at the same time, I thought it was what all men liked, and that I should exclusively please them.

Erika's husband Tom told me that he can't stand that position. It makes him feel like a weird, lifeless fish; he hates not being in control, and worries he is being lazy, and all of this prevents whatever is physically happening – even if everything is rubbing where it should rub – from working for him. This was a revelation; I felt completely the same in reverse. Even if my clit and G-spot were getting all the right attention, even if I was happy the guy was happy, even if I was enjoying seeing myself as the apparent modern iteration of sexy . . . it just couldn't get me there. Doggy style, legs-on-the-shoulder-folded-in-half, being bent over a sofa (being bent over anything), being pinned against a wall, being held against a basin: I could come from all of these. Even in vanilla sex, long before playing with anything 'kinky', I apparently needed that feel of submission, just as Tom needs that feeling of dominance. For me, the messaging around 'cool women being in control in the bedroom' had made me stop listening to my own mind and body. I felt the same way when I saw a book called *Don't Hold My Head Down* by Lucy-Anne Holmes. Please *do* hold my head down, everyone! (*Don't Hold My Head Down* is, in fact, a brilliant book. Rather than spending her twenties fake-enjoying cowgirl, Lucy had spent them pretending to enjoy all the positions I like, and she goes on an amazing journey to discover what she actually finds arousing, ignoring all the 'shoulds' she had previously heard.)

Ultimately, empowerment has nothing to do with what sex looks like, and everything to do with what is inside your mind and going on in your body. Having said all this, I discovered there is one very good way for me to get off on being on top. And that is to be ordered to do it, against my will – ideally with an audience.

❧

Torture Garden is everyone's first fetish night. It must be the most globally renowned fetish brand, and even people who have no interest in ever going to it are still likely to have heard of it. It has been running in London for over thirty years, which is no mean feat in a city where ordinary bars have a tough time staying the right side of stringent, nightlife-unfriendly licensing laws. So many people credit the night with being where they first began to find a place of acceptance and a community of like-minded people.

I didn't know what to expect before my first visit. We pored over the galleries on the website, trying to get a sense of it. The outfits looked so amazing. We realised we needed some latex.

How did latex become inextricably linked with fetish? What is so special about this material? If you see a latex outfit, it immediately signifies 'kinky sex' – and the material is used to that effect in music and fashion all the time.

We learned that in London, the Holloway Road is the home of designer latex. There are several shops, like Atsuko Kudo, whose creations are individual works of art. They were also far, far beyond our price range. We found there was a much more budget-friendly latex and leather shop in Lower Marsh Street, and headed down there one Saturday afternoon.

Heading up a discreet staircase, we found a small room with rows of hangers bearing items not easily identified as clothes. We told the assistant we were going to Torture Garden, and she showed me various latex options – skirts, hotpants, dresses, corsets. I took a pile into the changing room. She showed me how to use talcum powder on the inside of the clothes to stop them sticking to themselves and to me, and demonstrated how I could then coat the outside with a special latex spray to make it shiny and wet looking.

I tried on a long-sleeved midi dress, struggling into it and unravelling it slowly over my limbs. I immediately felt enclosed and restrained; there was something innately submissive just about the sensation of the material on my skin. I came out and looked in the mirror. It was extremely flattering, pulling in my waist and pushing out my boobs, and it smoothed the lines of my body. Even with no make-up and bare feet, I felt instantly like a fetish alter-ego of myself. That is presumably what the compulsory costumes at Torture Garden are for; it's such an obvious and easy way to discard your day-to-day self.

I tried on the various options. In the end, with a lot of advice from Max and the assistant, I went for a mini-skirt, which was fully cut away at the front, and a bra top. Lovely as the long-sleeved options looked, they seemed too hot for a club night, and as Max pointed out, were harder to get in and out of. He went for a pair of leather trousers and a leather harness to wear over his bare chest.

On the night, we arrived in a taxi at the big club – somewhere we had been many times on 'ordinary' club nights. It was strange to see the queue in elaborate latex, leather and burlesque outfits instead of the usual combats and trainers.

Once inside, we decided to explore to get a sense of the layout. There seemed to be a couple of large dancefloors, already a seething mass of movement. At a glance, it was like any dancefloor, but then, as the lasers and strobes illuminated the crowd, you realised you were in an alternate universe. There were pole-dancers on platforms and in dangling cages. On a stage, a hooded, topless man was performing elaborate shibari on a tiny dancer who was suspended aloft.

We continued on to find the famous dungeons. We crept in, and an amazing scene confronted us. There were so many different pieces of apparatus on which to be restrained, and in so many different positions – I had no idea what they were all called. I was puzzled at first by a coffin-shaped piece of equipment around which three people were standing. I realised they were putting their hands into strategically placed holes in the wood, and that there was someone inside. I gazed at it, fantasising.

Max shook his head in laughter. 'You are *so* predictable, Sonnet.'

In the middle of the room was a giant St Andrew's cross: an X-shaped iron structure, maybe eight feet tall. A woman was attached to it face down, her legs and arms strapped so she was completely spread apart. An audience had gathered in a semi-circle in front of it. Max and I weaved to the front, curious to see what was happening. We heard it first – a crack, which seemed to reverberate around the dungeon walls. A burly man, masked, topless, was pacing around the cross, holding a long, Indiana Jones-style bullwhip.

'Fuck,' I said.

The girl stopped screaming and writhing. The man walked up and whispered something in her ear. She smiled and closed her eyes; it was strangely intimate. He stepped back a few paces and unleashed the whip again. I saw it connect with her back, lacerating the skin. We watched in awe.

The dom went to untie his prey. She thanked him and rearranged her clothes, then someone handed her a drink and she merged into the crowd.

He looked around, enquiringly. Max immediately pushed me forward. I was about to protest, but there was something urging me on. The man took my hand, and led me to the cross.

'Wait,' said Max. 'Give me your knickers.'

I had worn a small thong under my latex skirt, as my cunt was fully visible thanks to the cutaway front half. Max knew that without the knickers, spread on the cross, the whole audience would be able to see it.

I obediently handed them over. The dom helped me step up forwards, high onto the cross, and positioned my legs and arms, strapping them in tightly. Every movement was deliberate and theatrical; this was for an audience, which made me even more aware of their presence. He tucked my skirt up into its waistband so that my arse and my cunt were fully exposed. My latex bra only had a thin strap at the back, so I was very conscious that the whole of the skin on the back side of my body was open to him. I felt the crowd hush, so I knew he must have stepped back into position.

I felt the first stroke land in my brain first, with the crack, and then immediately felt a shooting, searing pain across my butt cheeks. I was tied so tightly I couldn't writhe around much, but I was aware I was arching my back in convulsions with the shock. I had no time to think, and I couldn't form conscious thoughts anyway. Five more strokes rained down, on my back, my thighs, my arse. The whip seemed to reach such a large area, it was hard to tell where exactly it had landed. It was over very quickly, and it was a blur. The man untied me and helped me down.

'Well done,' he said.

I thanked him. Max took me out into the bar and we got a drink. He examined the marks.

'Jesus, it will be a miracle if these don't scar!' he said, seemingly delighted.

My skin was on fire. I was also aware that I had not been given back my knickers, so my cunt was on view to everyone.

We continued our explorations. We found a room hidden by a green curtain. Unlike the dark dungeon, the walls were white, and it looked like a hospital. There were medical green screens, and in the corner there was a Victorian medical chair – it was covered in cream-coloured, well-worn leather, with stirrups and straps. It made you think immediately of hysterics, asylums, and creepy medical institutions from the past, all of which were favourite fantasy settings of mine. Since visiting the preserved nineteenth-century operating theatre in the old St Thomas's hospital, I had frequently imagined myself strapped to its table, having 'operations' demonstrated upon me in view of all the curious students. When I learned that Freud, when he was positing his 'seduction theory', would have had me institutionalised as a hysteric, I repaid him with elaborate fantasies of being forced to recount my darkest desires naked on a couch, while *fin de siècle* Austrian psychiatrists 'tested' the scale to which I was aroused.

There was no one else in this secret medical room. It was tucked away off a staircase, and it was still early, so maybe people hadn't yet found it.

Max led me over to the medical chair and I climbed in, lying down on my back with my legs in the stirrups. He looped up the leather straps around my torso and secured them tightly, then attached the ankle straps. Then he moved the stirrups apart so my cunt was stretched open. He thrust his fingers inside. I so much loved feeling completely at his mercy, that I forgot where we were. Possibly so did he, as he unzipped his leather trousers, pulled out his cock and began to fuck me. We were in our own little world, deep inside the belly of the club.

After that, we decided to seek out the famous 'couples' room' – the designated sex space. We later learned you are not supposed to fuck in the BDSM rooms, a rule based on the idea that 'sex and BDSM are not the same'.

There was a queue leading to a mysterious curtained-off area. As we waited, we got chatting to other people. Eventually, we were allowed inside. There was a big, red round bed in the centre, filled with writhing bodies still partly clad in leather and latex. It was dark, barely lit. We could hear bodily fluids and the sound of skin on skin.

We found a space, and Max threw me down, immediately pulling off his trousers. He was hard again, and he thrust straight into me, pulling my ankles onto his shoulders. I could see people around watching us; so much of this night felt like being in a play.

We spent the rest of the night alternating between dancing and dungeon, making some new friends, watching performers and feeling like we had been initiated into a secret universe.

We left just as the sun was rising outside, and agreed we would probably come back.

❧

Anthony told me about his first experience caning a woman. I was kneeling at his feet, naked except for high heels, which were digging into the new welts on my arse, intrigued to hear the story.

In his early thirties, he had been living on the west coast of Spain. It was a time of liberalism and hedonism in a country still coming to terms with its new identity after forty years of fascist rule.

Anthony met Eloise in a bar on the coast, in the wonderful, louche hours between midnight and breakfast. He described her as perfect. A little older than him, elegantly windswept, tanned, long dark hair moving in the pre-dawn breeze, dark eyes that calmly dared you, a loose white linen shirt occasionally showing casually fabulous breasts, cut-off denim shorts. She had an easy laugh that gave you the sense that she had seen it all, and found it all amusing. She was French.

On his motorbike, they went back to her house, which turned out to be an architect-designed Malibu-style beach-front mansion. He had been slumming it, travelling and staying in cheap hostels; this was like nothing he had ever experienced.

He stayed for weeks. They fucked all day and all night. In the morning, two women would be dropped off in a clattering Renault. They would clean the house and prepare lunch, leaving it in the kitchen for them. Anthony and Eloise would eat on the terrace looking out to the sea, then sleep and fuck again in the afternoon.

The way he described it sounded like a beautiful, heady dream. The perfect, intense summer fling.

The way they were fucking was physical and vigorous. He would spank her, and she seemed to love it. She would be aroused by a slap to the face.

One day, she said she needed him to do something for her. She went to the wardrobe and came back with a cane. She held it out to him on open palms, and said, 'Please.'

He told me that even then, it had been something lurking in his mind; it was already there, somehow, but he had never considered suggesting it or thought it would ever happen.

He said, 'I took the cane from her, and suddenly felt like we were engaged in some ancient ritual. It felt completely right in my hand. I told her to bend over the bed. I let the end of the cane stroke her round, tanned bottom gently. I could smell how wet she was. I tapped the skin and watched the small ripple of impact. I wanted the first stroke to be right: hard and well-aimed. I concentrated on the action, the placement of the mark, then raised the cane high and brought it down fast, following through. She didn't scream but gasped, as if in amazement, and bent her knees. I told her to stay still. I noticed my cock was rock hard.'

Afterwards, they fucked and it sounded like a next level experience, she rode his cock, one orgasm endlessly tumbling into the next, for ever.

After that, cane stripes became a regular feature of Eloise's arse and thighs. She would walk along the beach in a thong bikini, showing them off. Anthony would watch from the terrace as everyone stared. Some people were clearly outraged, some men leered and made crass jokes, some people were embarrassed and looked away, and a few women came up to her and asked about the marks in curiosity.

I loved this origin story, and I was intrigued about Eloise's pride in the marks. Anthony often canes women for photography; the marks are the most important aspect, as it is all about how they will look in the pictures. He tends to get models approaching him who are curious about it, as the marks feature so prominently in some of his work. Sometimes things evolve further than photography and become about the experience, as they had with us, and sometimes they didn't.

I liked seeing marks on my skin. It was somewhere between an exhibitionistic pride – *Look what I can do!* – and an arousing humiliation. To be marked by someone's force upon you is like being branded; it signifies ownership, deference, submission. Max would inspect the marks as they developed and changed shape and colour, loving the physical reminder of my sluttiness and surrender to another partner. In particularly energetic phases, I would have welts and bruises from multiple participants, mingling in a beautiful collage, causing one dom to ask me if he would ever get a chance to play on some pristine virgin skin again.

But I went to great lengths to hide the marks outside of my kink world. I would start changing uncharacteristically modestly at the gym. I would wear long trousers if my legs were marked, and high-necked tops if my neck was. I have never got very into swimming, despite liking the feel of water and my love of all physical activities; my skin would be too much on display. I was careful about when I scheduled activities; there were many times I would have loved to have seen Anthony, but I was going on holiday and wanted to wear a bikini, or had a wedding coming up where my dress was backless, or a festival where I had planned to wear hotpants.

I knew the marks would cause disapproval or questions, or make people gossip behind my back. Once, I hooked up with a beautiful Italian man on a work trip. We tumbled back to my hotel, and when we were naked, he suddenly jumped back saying, 'Woah, what the fuck happened to your back?' I had completely forgotten there were lingering whip marks from a fortnight earlier. I had to explain, and it did rather upset proceedings, as I think he then thought I would only be turned on if he went full dom, which just wasn't him. That wasn't the case at all; I'd been expecting a lovely, hot, sexy, fun one-night stand. It's hard to explain that just because BDSM turns me on, that doesn't mean vanilla sex cannot.

Once, Anthony announced that he was going to give me a red dress. I had to stand in the middle of the room, and from my tits to my knees, he went all over my skin – back, front, sides – with the evil jelly fish flogger. By the end, it did indeed look like I was wearing a red tube dress. We have some excellent photos. The dress was solidly purple the next day, and then it became a crochet of yellow and brown. I loved my dress.

❧

As I began to play with more and more physical expressions of submission, different kinds of restraint and pain, I realised that surprisingly, maybe, it was making me feel physically strong. I discovered my body's capability for healing bruises quickly, but more fundamentally, I could also see that this play was making my muscles stronger and more flexible. Jordan had upped the ante since that first non-monogamous night years earlier, and loved to have me balance on his four high, round, leather-covered barstools, one for each knee, and one for each elbow. To stop myself from faceplanting down to the ground, I had to use my deepest core strength, with my hamstrings, quads and adductors fully engaged. He would push a heavy stainless steel dildo into my cunt and make me hold it there with my pelvic floor muscles. All of this would then be challenged by being flogged and spanked, and fingered or fucked in the arse. Potentially for an hour. Eat your heart out, Crossfit.

Poorna Bell writes in her brilliant book *Stronger* about how women are not taught they can be physically strong – if you say 'a strong woman', we immediately think of a *resilient* woman, someone who has come through mental challenges, maybe, or is admirably dealing with stressful family situations, work or illness, rather than someone who can bench-press. By contrast, if you refer to a man as 'strong', you often mean it more literally. She explains how interconnected physical strength is to empowerment. As we age, particularly, the messaging seems to be that self-care is all about bubble baths and making time for a nice lie-down. But I think the danger in this can be that we start to see ourselves as porcelain dolls, so easy to break. We may now know that 'the body keeps the score', but this does not mean that women's bodies are so precious and delicate. To me, that message seems to take us back to the nineteenth century, when we would apparently get 'brain fever' for six months after being caught in a brief rain shower. If we are told we are physically weak, we will believe it. I was not trying to prove my strength through physical submission – but it was increasingly a happy by-product. And in feeling the power of my body, I felt more powerful emotionally.

Max and I were in New York. It was a brutal winter, one of the coldest on record, and the whole of the US had been ravaged by icy storms.

Cold is one physical sensation for which I had nothing but contempt. It was a nuisance, to be overcome by clothes, central heating and movement. I loved being out in the snow – if I was wearing several thermal layers and snow-shoeing up a hill. I could plunge myself into cold Atlantic waves – if the sun was warm enough to bask on the beach immediately afterwards. Winter was about curling up by fires with sheepskin rugs and warming red wine. But navigating normal city life, when you had to wear so many layers and carry so many things around, was cumbersome. It made me feel trapped, and like my naked body was so far away from other people. I was pining for those humid NYC evenings that stay sticky and sultry until past midnight, and seem full of anticipation; nights when people catch each other's eyes and notice each other's skin, rather than bowing their heads against the howling wind and scuttling along the sidewalk as fast as the ice allows.

Max thought my cold-bashing was ridiculous. He had an internal body temperature like an NYC apartment's heating: non-adjustable and always set to max. In our draughty London flat, when I went to bed in a tracksuit and two pairs of socks, he would look at me in bemusement. 'Why can't you deal with this?' he would ask, his hands all toasty, while mine had gone from blue to white, and I wondered if this time I would actually lose a finger.

So it was with a particularly evil and gleeful glint in his eye that he told me about Dave. Dave was a photographer Max had found on one of the fetish photography websites, and he specialised in pictures of naked women around New York. Some of his photos were nonchalant nudes – a beautiful woman reclining on a pavement café seat, drinking an espresso, completely naked, as the city seemed to bustle around her unconcerned, or three naked women on the subway. Some were kinkier – women tied by the neck to street furniture, peeing in public, wearing hoods in the street. They were all great photos, black and white with an air of city reportage, though they must have been carefully staged.

'You should shoot with him. I got his number; I said you would message.'

I had a moment of exasperation at his going ahead and arranging things for me, immediately followed by a submissive wave of excitement in my body and my cunt.

'OK, give me my phone . . .'

Dave got back to me quickly. He texted like a normal person – or as normal as you can sound when you are asking people whether they are OK with outdoor bondage and public nudity. But he sounded very professional, and as if he was all about the photography, not about the kink. I liked this – I found that sometimes I got off on the fact that while the photographer was being business-like on a shoot, all about the art, I was getting turned on by being exposed and bossed around.

Dave wanted to meet at 5.30 a.m. the following Tuesday, when it would still be dark and the streets empty, and shoot in five different locations as the sun came up. He finally addressed the elephant in the room, writing: 'You know it's going to be fucking cold? How are you with that?'

I read this aloud to Max. He grabbed the phone from my hands and replied for me: 'Oh, I'll do what I'm told.'

The night before the shoot, I realised I was not nervous about being shit at modelling, about being naked in public, or about the safety of doing an intimate shoot with a stranger . . . but I was terrified of the cold. Our apartment was boiling, and I slept naked so as not to get any clothing marks on my skin, but I tossed and turned all night, worrying about my imminent hypothermia.

My alarm went off at 4.45 a.m. and I made coffee, put on some make-up, and then layered up in the loosest but warmest clothes I could find, along with big, furry snow boots, ski mittens and a bobble hat. Max woke up to see me off and had immediate hysterics.

'Sexy outfit there, Sonnet!'

'I can't believe you are doing this to me. There'd better be a hot bath followed by an excellent breakfast when I get back,' I replied brattily.

He kissed me goodbye. 'Be good, keep your phone on. Text me updates.'

I went downstairs. The icy air immediately hit me through my big coat and layers. Dave had arrived on a vintage Vespa in some extremely warm-looking leathers, and a pair of big gauntlet gloves that I found somehow arousing. He was very tall and broad with long hair, and had the air of having been in a biker gang at some point. He handed me a helmet, which had a handy internal microphone so we could talk to each other. I got on the back of the Vespa and we pulled off into the sleety streets. I had the by-then familiar feeling of 'Life really is weird and wonderful', a sensation that is one of the life-affirming side effects of all slightly bizarre endeavours.

As we pulled out onto the West Side Highway, the wind whipped off the Hudson, lifting drifts of snow into the air. Fortunately, Dave's body shielded me from the elements, and I was distracted from the cold by the beauty of the desolate, pre-dawn city. We chatted through the headphones about his life in New York, and he told me what he was thinking for the shoot.

The first stop was a giant Christmas tree down in the financial district. My knowledge of that part of the city was still hazy, but we seemed to be far south, amongst the banks and law firms. We parked the Vespa and walked over. Dave explained that he wanted me to lie over a big rock in front of the Christmas tree, naked except for high heels, which he had brought, with my arse in the air.

We did some practice shots with me still clothed. Even through my coat, I could feel the cold granite. He looked around. There were a few workmen about, and what looked like some traffic cops.

'We'll have to be quick, but it should be fine.'

It was the first time it had occurred to me that being naked in public was a crime, in a country where owning a gun was not. But I figured busting UK citizens out of jail for nude modelling in Manhattan is just what the British Embassy is for.

'OK, are you ready?'

We snuck down into someone's basement fire escape and I undressed, with Dave deferentially looking in the other direction. I then put only my coat back on, and the heels. He took up his position with his camera.

'OK, when you're ready.'

I threw off my coat, and scuttled to the rock. The air was an instant plunge-pool shock, and my skin was immediately on fire. I bent over the rock and the cold granite pierced me. I listened to his instructions – legs open, legs closed, back arched, bum up – just audible over the wind, and then, so quickly, he told me to get up.

I kicked off the heels and ran back naked over the plaza towards him. He was holding my coat, and I struggled into it, and then he put his arms round me. I had that wave of post-adrenaline parasympathetic nervous system euphoria and release, which I associated with being caned. It was heady and amazing, and made me like Dave a lot.

'Are you OK? That was great!'

I laughed that it was. I marvelled – had he somehow managed to kinkify being cold? My curiosity about this took over. I fleetingly wondered if Wim Hof addressed this in that book everyone is always reading about the health benefits of rolling around in ice.

The next shoot required a bit more bravado on my part. We Vespa-ed up to the famous Katz's Delicatessen in the Lower East Side. The sun was up, though the light was so cold and grey you could barely tell. More people were around, and the roads were getting busier with commuters.

Dave's idea was to have me hang naked from a high traffic light, in front of the shuttered deli, so the sign was in the background behind me. We practised fully clothed. It involved climbing up onto a fire hydrant, then reaching for the crossbar of the traffic light, swinging onto it, then hanging down. Even with gloves on, the metal of the bar was very cold to grasp.

At almost 7 a.m., Houston Street was getting busy. We were going to have to time the shots with the traffic, since Dave had to be in the middle of the road. There were quite a few people around, including a man painting the signage on the adjacent shopfront. He gave us a cheery wave as we worked out the logistics and choreographed the timing.

Then, once again, I undressed modestly in an alcove, and emerged with just my coat. This shot was to be barefoot, and the icy feel of the concrete was curiously similar to the sensation of boiling sand on the soles of your feet on a very hot beach. I walked back over to the intersection, and we waited for the right moment in the traffic sequence. When it came, I threw off my coat, Dave ran into the street, and I climbed on the fire hydrant, leaping for the lights crossbar. I dangled like a naked trapeze artist, trying not to giggle hysterically at the absurdity of the whole thing. Dave took quick burst shots as I stared in various directions and tried to look nonchalant, gripping onto the metal bar even though it felt like it was blistering the skin on my hands.

The lights changed and I dropped down, miraculously not spraining my ankles, and grabbed my coat from the ground.

I looked around. Several people were going about their business, seemingly unfazed by the sight of a naked woman hanging from a bar high above the major east–west thoroughfare. The painter, however, had given up any pretence of not staring at us. He climbed down from his ladder and as we walked past, he said, 'Thanks guys, that has really made my morning.'

As we got back on the Vespa, Dave asked if I was sure I was OK, since I was shaking and shivering a lot. I said I thought it was the adrenaline as much as the temperature, and that I was enjoying it all immensely.

The next stop was Freeman Alley – a passageway that had been given over to street artists and was filled with all kinds of colourful graffiti. I had been to the trendy restaurant at the end of the passage a couple of times, but it looked very different closed up this early in the morning.

Halfway along the passage, there was a high wrought-iron railing and gate, which formed the entrance to a boutique hotel. The hotel was very much open, and the reception staff could probably see, but aside from them, the alley was quiet.

Dave's ideas for this shot were a bit kinkier. He wanted me to be tied to the railings in a cross, my arms and legs outstretched, with a black hood over my head, and big pegs on my nipples and labia. This was hard to practise in clothes, so I got naked for the set-up. He asked if I wanted to place the pegs myself, which felt amusingly gentlemanly for the scenario, but I replied that I was completely fine with him doing it. The alley was at least sheltered from the howling wind, and I was quite numb by this point, so getting undressed seemed less heart attack-inducing this time.

I climbed naked onto the front of the railings, and Dave took out his ropes and tied my wrists to the bars. He gently moved my legs apart and tied my ankles to the rails as well. He put the hood over my head, and the world went dark. Mostly it made my head warm, which was nice. He looped the rope around my neck, very loosely, then more tightly around my mouth over the material, like a gag. He kept checking I was OK, but it was a bit difficult to affirm that in my bound condition. I could easily still breathe through my nose, though, so I was quite comfortable.

I felt him pinch my frozen nipple, presumably to get it ready for the peg, and despite the cold and the awkward position, I felt a wave of arousal. By the time he had pegs on both nipples, I could feel my cunt like a throbbing warm heart, in contrast to the rest of my body, which seemed to be going into a cryogenic coma. He reached down to place the pegs on my labia, and I knew he must be able to see that I was wet, since my legs were spread wide apart. If he did, he didn't comment.

Finally, everything was ready, and I heard him moving around me and the shutter clicking. It was quite peaceful here in the alley, in my hood, and the sounds of the city seemed distant.

'You are actually turning blue,' Dave said, and set about untying me.

Somehow, on being released, I realised just how cold I was. I got dressed again very quickly. I was shaking wildly and started desperately doing star jumps to get my blood pumping. This was somehow too funny, and the thought of anyone watching the scene had us both in fits of laughter.

'Let's just do one more, if you think you can manage it?'

'I can, I can,' I said, adding some squat jumps to the alleyway HIIT routine I had going.

At the entrance to the passage, where it met the main road, there was a low gate with more convenient iron railings. It was about as high as my ribs. Dave explained he just wanted me to be bent over it, legs spread, ankles and wrists tied together through the bars, arse in the air – clearly a favourite pose of his.

I climbed into position, feeling oddly proud of the flexibility that allowed me to do exactly as he commanded. The top bar of the gate dug into my stomach, and as he lifted my feet off the bottom rung to be tied to my hands, I realised I would have to engage my core so as not to faceplant and break my nose. I wondered if 'balancing naked over a gate' could become the new abdominal workout trend.

I was in position quickly, and he stepped back and took photos. At that moment, a few people emerged from within the passage – maybe they were coming from the hotel. A small elderly woman in a long fur coat and fur hat, looking so completely 'New York', stopped to survey us. Then she walked right up to me, and bent down to my face

'Is everything OK here, hmmmm?' she demanded.

I smiled at her as best I could, upside down and tied up. 'Yes, it's just a photoshoot, all fine.'

'Humph,' she said, and scowled at Dave as he smiled at her, pausing to let her pass.

What a great city, I thought. Where else would an excellent, bold, older woman pause to double-check you're not being raped or abducted in a public street at 8 a.m.? Even though nothing about the shoot had felt in the least scary, it was nice to know there were strangers looking out for me, although she would no doubt later use the story as an example of how the neighbourhood had gone to the dogs. In London, everyone is too awkward and embarrassed to approach; months later, Dave and I shot around Waterloo Station at 10 a.m. on a Sunday, and when people happened to pass, *they* apologised to *us*.

I got dressed quickly, and as I replaced my hat, Dave nodded in the direction of a café directly opposite the gate. One of New York's Finest was emerging with a polystyrene coffee cup and a doughnut, making me feel even more like I was in an increasingly surreal TV show. He got into his patrol car, which had been parked only metres from us throughout proceedings.

'That was close,' said Dave. 'Right, I think we really have to call it, as otherwise I'll have to take you to the ER.'

I protested, but his good sense prevailed. I texted Max, dropping large hints about bubble baths and hot coffee.

It was now full-on rush hour, and the streets were busy as we threaded through the traffic. I hugged Dave tightly for warmth, and in affection – the kind that doms so often inspire in me. This might sound like a strange response to someone who causes you pain and humiliation – and frostbite – but it feels natural to me. It's the warm feeling of joyous amazement that there are other freaks like you out in the world, people who want to play with you, who don't think it's at all odd that you would want to drive round Manhattan on a snowy winter morning creating kink art. Everyone feels happy when they make a new friend who gets them, and that is immediately what I felt with Dave.

I handed back the helmet and hugged him goodbye, and he promised to share the pictures soon. I climbed the stairs to our apartment and heard the water running. Max opened the door and handed me a coffee, shaking his head. 'You're crazy!'

I thawed out in the bath, and realised I had the kind of hunger possibly only sub-zero al fresco fetish modelling can inspire. We went out for pancakes, and I told Max all about it.

❧

Frederik messaged to say he was in the lobby, identifiable by the long, thin object wrapped in blue cloth he was carrying. I went down to meet him wearing a very short sweater dress with bare legs and the hotel flip-flops on my feet, my stomach doing somersaults and my heart racing. He was very tall and looked strong, and was old enough to have a kind of world-weary air of experience that I found terrifying and reassuring in equal measure.

We got into the lift and I tried to make normal conversation, but my mouth was dry. It felt far more deviant to invite a stranger to one's hotel room at 9 a.m., before work, than it did to sneak in the more traditional late-evening guest. I unlocked my door and we went inside. He surveyed the luxury hotel room, commenting that there was, at least, some floor space. As he put down his bag and took off his coat, he told me to kneel down. Having unwrapped a photographic light and a cane and placed them on the table, he looked down at me and said, 'So, you think you need to be punished?'

I nodded, if somewhat hesitantly.

'Why is that?'

I said I didn't know. I knew these answers were quite shit, but I was too nervous and excited to be coherent.

'Have you always wanted to be punished?'

I nodded again, thinking how true that really was.

'OK,' he said. 'Are there any no-nos?'

I shook my head – I can never think of any – before remembering how I had gone to my work meetings with bruises all over my chin and throat after happening to meet a dom in NYC recently. So I said, 'Maybe no face.'

He nodded. 'If it gets too much, really too much, you say, "I can't take any more," and I will stop. Otherwise, I don't stop. Can you remember that?'

I said yes, feeling completely determined that there was absolutely no way I was going to say that sentence, whatever happened. He turned away to get out his camera and other items. I reflected that there was something so excellent about a Scandinavian accent, lilting and menacing at the same time.

He showed me a strange leather device with a long, thick loop. 'Do you know what this is?'

I shook my head.

'You will find out later. It is worse than a cane. Well, so I am told. I wouldn't know.'

He lifted me up by my chin and told me to walk around to the other side of the bed. Then he told me to kneel down and put my face on the ground and my arse in the air. I tried to arch my back as much as possible and show how keen I was to be obedient, and hoped that I looked pretty to him from this angle.

'So did you sleep well last night?'

I said no, not at all; I had spent the whole night a ball of nerves and excitement.

'And how many times did you make yourself come, thinking about today?'

'Several,' I mumbled, thinking he somehow knew me – or, at least, people like me – very well.

He lifted my dress up over my bottom. I immediately felt my cunt twitch, and my face blushed into the rug at the thought of how easily someone I'd just met could turn me on, simply by exposing me. He took some pictures.

'You know I am going to really hurt you, don't you?' he said.

He pulled off my knickers and turned my head to the side so he could stuff them into my mouth. Then he pulled my legs further apart and took pictures of my exposed cunt. This had the effect of making it very wet. I knew he would be able to see this, which made it even wetter.

'You are getting excited already, I can see,' he said, confirming this. 'When were you last fucked?'

I truthfully answered, 'Saturday.' I had texted a local friend a naked selfie at 2 p.m. and suggested he come to my hotel room. There had been a knock at the door half an hour later, and I'd answered it in only my towel, dropping it when he kissed me. I remembered how desperate I had been to suck his cock when I felt how hard it was.

Frederik told me to get up and take off my dress, then moved me to kneel on the red velvet armchair. He pulled my bra down to expose my tits. He took some photos and then told me to take off my bra completely so I was naked.

'I think we will take some pictures of the blank canvas first.'

I mostly moved myself into the required positions, but even the slightest adjustment, his hands moving my thighs slightly further apart, was making me feel turned on, even though I knew these hands were about to cause some intense pain.

He told me to move onto the bed, calling me 'Sonnet-with-the-wet-cunt'. He took out the cane.

It had been a long time since I had been caned. I hadn't seen Anthony for three years, what with Covid causing work and family complexities, and us usually being in different countries. I had never found anyone else who was so into it – or to whom I could fully surrender and access that glorious full-body experience. I hadn't been seeking out pain, but recently life in general seemed to have come back with a vengeance, and with it a tingling sense in my skin. My epidermis was awakening and almost saying, *Give me to someone who knows what to do with me.* It was a physical itch for that unique feeling. Which is why when Max had spotted an Oslo-based photographer whose website had some stunning images and hinted at his expertise, I had decided to see if he wanted to shoot during my trip there. The only time we could make it work was this bizarre early-morning slot, but I found it was lending an even greater sense of surreality to the proceedings.

The first stroke was not that bad; I knew he was testing me. But the sound and the immediate sting, followed by the second-later afterburn, led to a kind of Pavlovian response of adrenaline and total arousal. I thought, *Oh, wow, this still really works on me.*

'What do you say?' he asked.

I gasped, 'Thank you.'

Of course, the strokes got progressively harder as I tried to show I could take more and he pushed further. If

I forgot to say thank you, he would slap me on top of the cane marks, which hurt so much, and if I couldn't hold my position he told me off, but it was so hard. He stopped to take photos and look at my teary red face, commenting that my mascara wasn't running, so I wasn't properly crying. He would either tell me I was a good girl and was doing well, or reprimand me for moving or not saying thank you.

He tapped the cane against my cunt. I knew he could see how swollen and sensitive it was. Then, completely unexpectedly, he slapped me hard on my cunt. I screamed out.

'You did not see that coming, did you?' he said, chuckling. 'Now, touch yourself. But you are not allowed to come until I say so.'

He took pictures as I put my fingers in my so, so wet cunt, and tried to not come immediately. If I stopped touching myself, he would tell me off. He said I needed to be on the very brink of coming, and whenever I was, he rained down the cane on my arse or spanked me again and again on top of the cane marks, which was somehow worse than the cane itself.

He asked me if my asshole was often fucked and said it should be, that it was a waste otherwise.

Finally, he said, 'OK, I am going to count to five, and you come on five. Not before. And if you don't, I will punish you badly.'

He counted down slowly, still hitting me, and I stopped holding back and came just about on time, rolling over and crying out as he took photos of me helplessly sprawled over the bed.

He gave me a glass of water and a little rest, but somehow made it clear this was very much only just the beginning. My arse was stinging and I was feeling pretty delirious.

He moved me to the red chair and had me kneel on it again, then caned me many, many more times. I was getting a bit unsure how much more I could take, but it also was releasing so many endorphins or dopamine or whatever strange brain chemicals seem to be accessed by the amazing combination of being completely at someone's mercy, the humiliation, the exhibitionism, and the pain itself. He picked up a hotel flip-flop, a surprisingly sturdy bamboo affair, and spanked me with that too, seemingly impressed with its results.

He sat on the bed and I knelt down on my heels in front of him. He looked at me, then roughly pinched my nipples, and pulled them hard.

'Oh, you hate this so much! I somehow knew you would,' he said, laughing.

They really did feel extra sensitive; my tits were all period-swollen, and my nipples feel like two extra clitori at the best of times, and at this point my senses were extremely heightened.

Next he took out the strange loop thing. It was apparently called a 'loopy johnny'. He showed it to me, and explained why the leather tube, stiff but more flexible than the cane, could inflict worse pain, in a double stroke. And it was conveniently portable. My heart raced. On top of my already nearly broken skin, this seemed very scary.

He bent me over the bed. After the first stroke, I pressed my face into the sheets and clenched my fists, trying to stay where I was, but it was so hard not to writhe in pain. He did a few more strokes, and it really was worse than a cane. He surveyed his handiwork and took photos.

He moved me to the wall and had me press my face and chest into it, then spread my legs and arch my back. He spanked me hard and observed with dispassionate interest that this seemed to be worse for me than even the loop. Finally, he gave me a choice of all three options, for one last round before I could have a break. Unbelievably, the cane seemed the least hideous. He said there would be five strokes – unless I moved from position, in which case there would be far more.

I flinched at the first.

'I'll pretend I didn't see that,' he said.

Somehow, I got through four more relentlessly hard strokes without falling down or falling apart.

He pulled me up and hugged me, and I felt a rush of love and humility and searing gratitude. It felt, as it always does, such an honour to be made to feel this way, and to find someone who not only connects immediately to the particular way in which my body is wired, but also gets off on it.

We ordered coffees from room service and relaxed on the bed, me naked and bruised and dishevelled, and him fully clothed. We talked about finding out about our predilections for respectively inflicting and receiving pain. Like all the doms I have ever met, he seemed to be a kind, intelligent, thoughtful and empathetic person.

A young hotel worker arrived with the coffee and looked a little awkward. He could probably see the cane and the photographic light and that I was in a dressing gown. Somewhat sadly, I didn't even find that particularly humiliating. I knew that ten years before, the presence of a hotel employee or any stranger witnessing any slutty or submissive behaviour from me would have caused my pulse to race and considerable shame and anxiety. Shame as part of play – the humiliating postures and practices, and feeling ashamed at how they turn me on within the context of the encounter – can become, if anything, more extreme with practice. The Pavlovian, automatic physical responses build and build, so now a tiny comment or a photo can transport me right back to a time when I was crawling around in the dirt, begging for mercy. But real-life embarrassment about kink has greatly waned for me over the years. For one thing, seeing how very many people are into it makes you realise it's less weird than you thought, but I think it's also simply part of growing older and deciding, *Who cares?*, as we do about a lot of things. Usually, if a random person stumbles into something, they are going to be far more embarrassed than you – but in the context of hotel rooms, I had come to realise, probably not at all surprised. Although this was probably emotional growth of some kind, I slightly missed the idea of being plunged into quivering fear due to the presence of a bell boy.

'Right, we do not have much time, and I am not finished with you,' Frederik said.

He put me over his knees, which is always such an intimate way to be spanked: pressed into a lap, feeling their cock or cunt beneath you, aware that they can feel all your shudders, and can hold you still. He spanked me hard, again and again. I lost track of the number of strokes.

We went back to the chair. This time, I was upside down over the back with my hands on the floor. The little break had made the stinging give way to a deeper, more bruised sort of pain, so when he started again, there was an extra level of depth. He made me touch myself again as he hurt me and photographed me. My cunt was throbbing and throbbing, as was my skin. He slapped me harder and harder, all over the cane marks. It was excruciating.

Eventually, he said, 'I think you might have had enough. Any more and you are going to bleed.'

I could only mutter, 'Maybe?', while thinking, *Ohhhh, thank god.* I was determined I was not going to be the one to call it. I fleetingly thought that if only I could exhibit this kind of grit and determination in other areas of my life, surely I would be an Olympic athlete or prime minister by now.

As we hugged, I clung on and thanked him – and I really meant it.

Frederik left and I showered, the water piercing my broken skin like knives. Afterwards, I went out to my work lunch. Walking there was a struggle, sitting even more so, and when someone suggested a glass of wine, I answered very vehemently, 'Yes.'

❧

Our very first act, when our skin hits the air outside the womb, is to take a breath. Is there anything more beautiful, then, than surrendering control of your breath to another person? It might be the most perfect kind of submission, offering up your very life force to someone else.

Like so many magical functions of being human, Western modern thought tends not to pay much attention to breathing until it 'goes wrong', as if this fundamental part of our existence is like a circuit on an electrical appliance, unnoticed until it malfunctions. But in other traditions, the mysteries of breathing and what we can do with it have been long celebrated. Becoming conscious of your breath, restricting it or changing its depth and speed in order to access other states of being, are central aspects of many ancient kinds of meditation, yoga and worship. It's thus not surprising how transcendental playing with breath can be during sex, and how many people love to do it.

I had long loved to be choked – and it must be one of the most common kinks. It's two-fold for me: the depiction of dominance cannot be clearer than hands round a neck, but I also love it for the moment when those hands squeeze and I feel the restriction of oxygen, first in the front of my head, then in my chest, then in my hands and feet as they begin to feel tingly and numb. A cock thrust deep into my cunt at that moment seems to access some other plane of existence, and if I come, it feels like a primeval force from a deep, ancient place. However, it only works with someone who really knows what they are doing. Choking is a detailed skill. Max read entire books about it, with great names like *The Loving Dominant*. He watched countless serious instructional videos. He practised on me carefully, getting my feedback, and only when he had felt like he had it down on me, would he ever suggest introducing it with anyone else – and with the full awareness that they might like it done differently to me. Sadly, a lot of men seem to think they are experts, having watched some fake choking in porn, and assume that all women like it. Nobody likes inexpert choking, to have their neck pinched and grabbed, the air not even constricted – or worse, something truly dangerous. Aside from your breath, this is your *neck*. You wouldn't trust someone who isn't a fully trained osteo to crack it, would you? And if you are not an osteo, you wouldn't go round giving neck adjustments. Even if you love to be choked, you will not like it being done badly. More importantly still: *lots of women do not like it and never will*. How this can be a surprise to anyone is beyond me. But it is widely reported that – probably in response to the prevalence of pseudo-BDSM porn, which mimics BDSM activities but is devoid of the connection and real surrender it requires – men are adding choking to the most vanilla of sex as if it's as basic as the missionary position. As with many kink activities, if I think someone isn't skilled and they are going for it as if they think they are, I will ask them to come back to me after a little more practice. For Max and for regular partners whom I trust, I am very happy to be their guinea pig as they learn something new, and to contribute to the safe upskilling of our nation.

Tom is a giant. It's like he is from a planet where everything is bigger and stronger. He is six foot seven, he can probably lift 180kg, and his cock is an absolutely terrifying prospect. He told me once that until his late twenties, he felt awkward about his size – he hated the idea that his physical being could be threatening, and he felt uncomfortably out of kilter with the world. Having only compared his cock with those in porn, he had no idea his was an extremely large specimen. He figured the women he slept with were just being nice. It was only when he moved to Portland and met Erika, and she introduced him to the wonderful world of polyamory and kink, that he began to see how to use his size and strength, how unique it is, and how many people love it. Being dominant is in no way about size, and the tiniest person can be the most menacing, but there is a particular kind of physical dominance that Tom really does very well.

One day I was thinking about deep-throating, and how I wasn't very good at it. My mouth is narrow top to bottom, and I found it physically hard, often worrying I wasn't doing a good job or that my teeth would catch. Max's response to most limiting beliefs is, 'Well not with *that* attitude,' and I realised I needed to approach the task with more of a growth mindset. I called Tom and asked if he would like to tutor me. Shockingly enough, he said he would embrace this commission with relish, but that I had to be extremely obedient and do everything he said without complaint.

For my first lesson, I arrived at his flat. He took me straight through to the living room and told me to take off my dress. I wasn't wearing any underwear, at which he nodded approvingly. He pushed me to my knees.

'Now, are you going to work hard and be a good student?'

I nodded.

'Wrists.'

I held up my wrists and he put leather cuffs on them, and then he pulled my arms behind my back and clipped the cuffs together.

'This is about your mouth, which you will submit to me, not about your hands.'

He unzipped his trousers and pulled out his gigantic cock, which was already hard. I remembered all the times I had been impaled upon it in the past and barely able to walk for days afterwards, and smiled at it fondly.

'Kneel up, and tilt your head back.'

I did, and could not resist moving my mouth towards his cock, but he slapped my face away.

'No. Did I tell you to do that?'

I knelt back.

'Now, open your mouth and keep your head still.'

He brought his cock towards my lips and I tried to open as wide as I could and to bring as much saliva as possible into my mouth. He dipped the tip in, as if just to wet it, and languorously moved it around inside my mouth.

'Relax your head, relax your jaw, stay *here*.'

He began to move my head back and forth, and I tried to be floppy and let go of the tension in my jaw. Only the very top of his cock was in my mouth, but it already felt like I was straining. However, as I really concentrated, I began to feel the stress in my tendons ease.

'Good. Good student. You can breathe here.'

I could, I realised. My mouth was full, but my airways were not blocked; I could breathe through my nose. I experimented with breathing slowly and calmly, and this helped relax my jaw.

He could feel this, I think, so he pushed in deeper. At this, I could feel my jaw clench again – and, indeed, my shoulders and possibly every other muscle in my body.

'I'm not going anywhere. We are staying here,' he said, beginning to thrust, but quite gently.

I could feel myself wanting to choke, but I concentrated on trying to find space for air through my nose and relaxing my jaw. My mouth filled with saliva. I wanted to swallow, but I couldn't. He could feel this.

'Uh uh, no swallowing. I want your mouth wet and I want your face messy. I want to see you dribble and to see my cock covered in your spit.'

My eyes were beginning to water, and I could feel saliva dripping out of the corners of my mouth and down my chin onto my exposed breasts. I could also feel my cunt throbbing, and it made me happy that my body was responding in this way. I genuinely wanted to learn something, I wasn't thinking about my own pleasure, but this was a happy side effect.

He began to thrust more urgently, and I began to move my head more in response. He let me. His cock grew even bigger, stretching my mouth, and I thought my face might tear, but I focused on not choking, not panicking, not pulling back. *RELAX*, I thought to myself, *and BREATHE.* I could just about get shallow breath though my nose into my lungs, though I could feel I was becoming slightly lightheaded. This was making me excited, which in turn was filling me with adrenaline, but I knew that wasn't what was needed. In *The Deepest Breath*, a Netflix documentary about free-diving, a diver moves from expert to champion when she figures out how to really relax underwater. When you slow your heartbeat, you can hold your breath for much, much longer. In his book *Teach Us to Sit Still*, Tim Parks has a host of horrible pelvic symptoms that cause him to be scheduled for a prostate operation, but when he learns how to breathe and properly, physically relax, all the symptoms disappear. If humans could do such amazing things, surely I could deep-throat a massive cock using the same techniques.

Tom looked me in the eyes and I somehow knew what was coming.

He pushed slowly inward, deeper, and then deeper. My mouth was so wet with spit that his cock moved quite easily to the back. Then, taking my head in his hands, he tilted it to the perfect angle and pushed down, down, down. I felt my throat bulge. I tried to take a breath, but there was no space for any air at all, so I suddenly panicked and choked and pulled back, coughing and crying and laughing.

'OK, it's a good start. We're going to try again. You can hold your breath much longer than that. Don't resist me. I'm in control, you can relax.'

All my many gym coach fantasies kicked in at that, and a spasm of excitement ricocheted through me.

'Ohhh, my student likes her lessons.' He reached down between my legs and pushed his fingers inside. I hadn't realised quite how aroused I was by this whole scenario. It turned out it was a lot. He thrust inside a few times, and then wiped his fingers all around my clit and labia. I moaned and nearly fell back from my kneeling position – my hands were still bound behind me.

He stopped and straightened up, and put his fingers in my mouth to clean them. 'Again.'

I obediently opened my mouth and he pushed in. This time, he went in deep to begin with. I could feel each thrust at the back of my throat, but I actively tried to drop my shoulders and unfurrow my brow, and with each exhale find the extra space. My jaw might be bone, but it is held together with skin, fascia, muscle, tendons and ligaments – and these are all probably elastic, I reasoned. I tried to visualise the inner workings of my throat and see everything softening and submitting, every cell's purpose being to accommodate his cock. I focused on sensation, the saliva making the skin around his shaft slippery and smooth, while everything inside was firm and meaty.

This time, when he began to push in deep, I exhaled completely. I was aware of how, as he reached the tighter places, the pressure made him harder. I could feel his cock swell inside the back of my mouth. As I felt it fill up my throat completely, my body felt quiet. There was an absence of air, and it felt like a calm moment, suspended in time. I swallowed, but didn't choke – and I felt his response to the sudden suction around his cock ricochet through his body. He pushed in further, slowly. I didn't want to breathe, and I didn't feel panicky. There was no wave of fight-or-flight adrenaline. It was like an offering. *I am yours*, I thought, and my eyes filled with tears at the beauty of this.

He pulled out and looked down at me with a proud teacher's smile, and as I gasped in air, he rubbed my clit and fucked me with his fingers until I came again and again.

We had a drink and a rest, but Tom made it clear that while our lesson might be over, he was not finished.

'You are an excellent student and an excellent slut, and I am going to make good use of you. You are my toy, and I am going to fuck you so hard, for as long as I want, and you will take it in your cunt like you have shown me you can with your mouth.'

I looked dubious. When he fucks me, it feels like my organs are actually being rearranged inside, my kidneys and liver all permanently misshapen.

He took me upstairs to the bedroom and told me to lie down, spread my legs and hold my cunt open for him. I cried out as he pushed into me. I was so turned on that my cunt was clenching around him, which actually made it harder for him to stretch me apart and push in.

'Toys don't make a noise,' he said.

I clamped my lips shut and tried not to cry out as he lifted up my legs and pushed his cock in deeper. That angle is excruciating with him, and I had to scream.

He shook his head and let my legs go, then leaned down and covered my mouth and nose with his hand, his cock still inside me. 'No screaming.'

Then, with my mouth and nose still blocked, he leaned his full weight onto my chest. I felt all the air squeezed out of my lungs. He was so strong, and I was completely compressed. He pressed harder and harder onto me. I felt I was being pressed through the bed, the floor, the Earth's crust, and down into a volcanic molten fire . . . At the same time, he pushed his cock in so, so deep. The sensation of being airless and pressed down and impaled all at the same time was intense. When he let me breathe, I came, hard, and he didn't move his cock out at all. It felt like there was no space to come, every crevice was full of his cock, which unbelievably still felt like it was expanding. I was somehow suspended in a continuous orgasm. Clearly, whatever my cunt was doing was having an effect on his cock, too. He was gasping, and then he pinned my shoulders down and fucked me hard for a minute before he came as well.

After we'd calmed down, I touched my sternum. It was tender.

'Wow,' I said, forever articulate. 'What the hell was that? It was amazing.'

'You *really* like having the air pressed out of you; the way your body responded to that was incredible. I could *feel* what it was doing to you. It was next level.'

'Let's do this again some time,' we both said together.

Erika, Tom's wife, came home a bit later, and we talked about asphyxiation. Her favourite thing to do with her submissive lover Jack is to sit on his face and to press harder and harder with her cunt so he cannot breathe. As a dom, she loves that feeling of ultimate submission, literally being trusted with his life, and she loves that it is her cunt that is the source of the power. She is less interested in choking with her hands. Jack sometimes ends up walking around with a swollen lip as a result, which pleases her too. I loved the idea that while Tom was choking me with his cock, Erika was choking Jack with her cunt. Somehow, we were all linked together with our breath.

I'm quite happy about the robots. What AI seems to be showing us is that the one small aspect of humanity we have for so long valued above everything else, and to the detriment of everything else – our capacity for cognitive thought – can be replaced. AI is already many times more 'intelligent' than us.

But AI cannot touch, taste or smell. It does not have an endocrine, muscular, respiratory or nervous system. Each of us hosts millions and millions of living creatures in our microbiome, like the galaxy contained in an orb on a cat's collar in *Men in Black* – and we don't need to mine the Earth's lithium reserves to feed them.

AI might be able to emulate creativity, but I think we're a long way from an Ishiguro robot who really can feel the sun on their skin and turn that feeling into a dance. Will 300,000 robots cry at 'Goodbye Yellow Brick Road' on the Pyramid Stage, or feel euphoria down to their toes when the beat drops at Fabric?

It's not an accident that as technology evolves, we seem to be evolving to celebrate the other parts of life. Interoception, mindfulness, yoga, nutrition, connection, breath, intuition, all things somatic: these are often cited as the balm to the stress of modern life, but I think they are a return to the 'deeper magic', as they say in Narnia, a lost, holistic way of appreciating all aspects of our minds and bodies and how we interact with each other.

So, until someone tasks AI with solving climate change, and it realises the inevitable conclusion is to eradicate humanity, let's celebrate our escape from the patriarchal, colonial tyranny of praising an ability to *think* above all, and look to the people who know how to *feel*.

I met Frederik by a large, hideously decorated Christmas tree in Oslo airport. He was quite smartly dressed and looked both relaxed and efficient, somehow. Obviously, I was terrified. Although my bruises from the first time we'd met three weeks earlier had faded, whatever neural pathways had been reactivated certainly had not, and I couldn't stop remembering the exquisite combination of pain and arousal; it had been scratching at the edge of my consciousness all the time. Which is why it had seemed like a sensible suggestion to ask if I could visit, and, when he suggested I spend the night at his house, to accept. I realised that a whole evening and night is significantly longer than the three hours we'd had before. He had warned me I would not get much sleep.

His instructions had included no orgasms for the last two days, but edging was permitted. I had to wear a short dress and stockings or tights I wouldn't mind saying goodbye to, white or bright panties, heels and runny mascara, and to bring a vibrator that reliably got me off. For some reason, I forgot the heels part, thinking of travel convenience. When I realised, my stomach lurched, thinking of what extra special punishment this might inspire.

We walked to the car park and got into his fancy car. As soon as we pulled on to the highway, he told me to pull down my tights, lift up my dress, pull my knickers aside and spread my legs. He looked at my cunt, which had been wet all day in anticipation.

He said, 'I gave you the right name last time I see, Sonnet-with-the-wet-cunt. Your cunt is going to get more attention this time.' I nodded obediently, even though it was a statement, not a question.

He turned on the inside light above me, which shone down, illuminating me. It was dark outside, and I felt very visible to everyone else driving through the evening rush hour. He told me to touch myself, but to stop on the brink of coming; I might be allowed to come at some point, but not for a long time, and certainly not without his permission. After I stopped, he took one hand from the wheel and pushed his fingers inside me, then squeezed my clit hard. He wiped his hand on my thighs and my face, while still looking at the road.

'I had hoped for more traffic,' he said.

I knew why – as the traffic was flowing, people were unlikely to look inside and see me exposed and wet.

'Now touch yourself again.'

We hit a traffic jam. On the right were lots of lorries, and I realised immediately that a driver would be able to look down and see my illuminated cunt if we were alongside them. We pulled up next to one.

Frederik looked up to see the driver. 'He's not looking,' he sighed, and then beeped his horn.

I felt my cheeks burn and drew my legs together.

'Open them,' Frederik admonished. 'Show him.'

I was mortified, even though I told myself, *What do I care what a stranger I will never see again may think?* I still felt humiliated, but I knew I had to be obedient.

As the traffic moved very slowly, we passed what felt like a never-ending procession of lorries, and each time we had the same routine: Frederik would not drive forwards till I had touched myself in a way they could see. One lorry driver beeped – in thanks? – as we pulled off. I felt like the people in all the cars around us could see what was happening too. In between lorries, he made me come to the brink of climax again and again, making me look at him and taking photos. He told me to look at the lorry drivers as I exposed myself to them. I looked up and made eye contact with one, then quickly looked away, ashamed, and gazed beseechingly back at Frederik.

Finally, the traffic started to move properly. As we pulled off the motorway, he disdainfully told me to pull up my tights and put my dress down. I was aware that my legs, and the car seat, were wet and sticky.

We pulled into a small, pretty road. He parked the car and we went into his house.

He directed me up the steep steps from the hall into a nice room with lots of books, a big rug and antique furniture. This immediately tapped into my many long-standing, if somewhat clichéd, 'professor-and-student' fantasies.

He told me to take off my dress and tights and to kneel on the carpet in front of a big swivel chair, which he sat down in.

'Now, before I inspect your bottom, we will have to order sushi,' he said, in what might be one of the great new literary aphorisms of our time. He reclined in the chair and looked at the menu while I knelt at his feet in my underwear, slightly shivering, though from cold or anticipation, I couldn't tell.

The order placed, he instructed me to get onto my hands and knees, then he pulled down my knickers and ran his hands over my arse.

'I can't see any marks. You have healed in three weeks – that's disappointing. This time will be much worse and last much longer.' He spanked me hard a few times, then got up and sat on the sofa. 'Over my lap. I know you think my hands are the worst of all, so let's start with that.'

I got up to walk over.

'NO. Crawl,' he said, exasperated. 'And if I do tell you to walk, it has to be on tiptoes, because you did not bring heels.'

I lay over his lap, my face turned to look up at him. He pressed on the small of my back. I knew that meant he wanted me to raise my arse up to him, to show I was eager to receive his punishment. He pulled off my bra and started to spank me, hard. With every stroke, I spasmed and my back rounded.

'NO. Keep, your position. You need training. Try. Again.'

I couldn't stop myself from flinching as each stroke was so powerful and his hands were so huge, but I at least tried to return to the correct position as quickly as I could.

'That is a little bit better,' he said, 'but you need much more training.'

As the strokes got harder, I pressed my face into the sofa in agony.

'No, I need to see your face and hear your whining.'

I was sweating and shaking and thinking, *Oh, there is so, so much more to come, will I be able to take it?*

He had me kneel on the ground and then he went into the next room. He came back and laid out a belt, a cane, the horrible loopy johnny, and a big flat slab of wood. He showed me this.

'It was supposed to be a keyboard wrist rest. I never used it for that,' he said.

'It looks very solid,' I said, looking at it dubiously. It was about a foot long, three inches wide, and nearly an inch thick.

'Later,' he said.

He told me to bend over the sofa and took up the belt. Each stroke stung and whipped in a double effect. As well as my arse and thighs, he struck my very tender cunt, hard.

His phone rang. The sushi delivery was outside.

'Stand up.'

I did, remembering to go on tiptoes.

'You are going to go down and collect it.'

'Noooo!' I cried, less bratty than begging. I was naked, my arse was burning and bruised, and my mascara, if not running in long streaks, was smudged all over my face.

'Go downstairs and get the sushi.'

I reluctantly walked down the stairs; he followed and sat on the top step, from where he could see the door. I protested again, but he ignored me. I fumbled with the door, and finally opened it just a little, quickly sticking my hand and face through the gap. I smiled at the delivery man and grabbed the bag, then slammed the door shut.

Frederik laughed in disbelief. 'That was pathetic. He saw what, your naked arm? Oh, you are going to be punished for this.'

'I know,' I said – and I did.

I wasn't really sure why I was so scared about a Deliveroo rider – like the lorry drivers, who cares? But something about the whole scenario had me exquisitely scared about everything. It was also partly about surrendering to Frederik – if I felt too blasé about submitting to his will, the whole set-up would crumble. It's like reading a book; we have to acquiesce and submit to the world the author is building. If we can't suspend our disbelief, the plot won't work. But there has to be willing on the part of the reader as well as the author; if you go into *The Lord of the Rings* with an attitude of, *But* why *do these creatures have big feet and live in hovels? It's not real!*, then the whole epic quest depicted in the novels is not going to feel like the searing, emblematic tale of good and evil it's supposed to be (and indeed, for many people, it does not). I am so happy for my emotions to be manipulated by authors that often I submit to it easily. The same is true in these long, immersive sessions; I buy into the fear wholeheartedly, feeling it throughout my body, because ultimately I know I love it. If part of the story is that I am scared of the Deliveroo driver seeing me naked, I will be scared of that. In this instance, it might have been better to be a little less scared, and to coquettishly dance out into the street – I can imagine doing that in another scenario, and I think it would have made Frederik chuckle – but on the other hand, if I'd done that, what excuse would he have had for my punishment?

Erika says that for her, the state induced by sex and kink is analogous to exercise and creating art. They are all ways to manipulate the nervous system into a flow state where we feel harmonised and alive. But these activities require bravery, commitment and serious effort. She's right, as any writer or athlete will tell you – things can be frightening, and they can be complicated and hard work, but they are so worth it.

*

Frederik and I went back upstairs and sat at the dining table. He opened a nice bottle of wine, and we could have been any normal people having dinner and talking about general things, except I was naked and he was clothed, my arse was throbbing, and I could feel my cunt every time I moved on the chair.

He seemed to be looking at my self-invented way of using chopsticks with some consternation. My hands were still shaking slightly, and pieces of sashimi kept falling back onto my plate. I laughed at myself, but then I looked at him and said, 'Can you teach me to do it properly?' I was enjoying his professor role too much to let it go.

He smiled and shrugged, and became the authoritarian version of himself again, albeit with a great tenderness. He gently positioned the chopsticks properly in the crease of my thumb and index finger, encased my hands in his, and lifted a gyoza to my lips. So many doms have this interplay of soft and brutal, the contrast making both so much more intense. It felt almost romantic, which somehow made the thought of what might be still to come even more exciting.

'You realise we have only just begun, don't you?' he said.

I nodded.

After dinner, we went back to the sofa. He had me stand up and bend down from my waist, my hands resting on a cabinet full of books. He took the cane and caned me ferociously and quickly so that the pain built up rapidly and there was no space for recovery, just as I remembered from before. I was using every muscle to try and stay in position and not move, but it was so impossible.

'I think it is time to try my new item. Lie over me.'

I was aware that there were so many welts and bruises forming, and that my blood was so close to the surface of my skin that everything would be extra bad at this point.

'Lift your arse up properly.'

I obeyed, tense with anticipation.

He brought the wooden plank down with a huge crack. I sprang forwards, screeching 'Fucking hell!', and then kind of crying-laughing at how intense it was.

He pulled me back. 'Ten.'

I shook my head no, but he held me down.

'Count.'

Somehow I got through the ten, crying out at each stroke. When he stopped, I clung onto him, shaking and burying my head in his shoulder.

'OK, ten more. You can do it.'

I knew there was no choice, so I lay down again and counted once more. This time it was even worse.

'You are a brave, good girl, even if you need training,' he said. 'Go and get a glass of water and kneel here.'

I did, kneeling on the floor in front of him, my heels digging into my arse and making me wince.

He let me rest for a while, and mused about how he was happy to have found a good use for the redundant wrist rest.

Then he laid out all the implements on the sofa, and made me choose one. I couldn't even think which was worst at this point. I hesitated, and finally went for the cane.

'Just five, each side,' he said.

On top of everything we'd already done, five hard strokes seemed like a huge amount. He sat down in the white swivel chair and told me to bring him a glass of wine, adding that I could have half a glass more.

I knelt in front of him.

'I have a present for you.' He got up and brought out a small hardback book: *Spanking the Maid* by Robert Coover. I admitted I'd not heard of it, and he said he thought I would like it. He asked me to read the first few pages aloud. They featured a maid, clearly trying to remember all the things her master had told her to do, as well as how she was supposed to behave as she was performing her servile tasks. I looked forward to reading the rest on the plane home. Of course, he had to spank me with it before he could give it to me: five hard strokes on each arse cheek. At this point, being spanked by a feather would probably have been excruciating, let alone a hardback.

He sat back in the swivel chair and told me to get my vibrator. I sat on the floor with my legs butterflied open, and he watched as I pressed the vibrator against my clit. I'd been in such a constant state of on-the-edge for hours, and I knew that if I was allowed to, I would come instantly. He pulled me closer and began to slap my face, hard. I gasped. For some reason, having my face slapped while my cunt is being touched or I am being fucked is the most guaranteed way to make me come immediately. Even when the slapping is really hard – and really hurts, as of course it did with *his* hands – it's so immediately and mechanically arousing that I love it, even in the moment. In fact, I had really been wanting to clearly retract the 'no face' request I'd made last time, as that had only been because I had to go to a meeting. I was delighted I didn't have to. I love the way that, as you connect more closely with a dom in an intense scenario like this, it can become a beautiful dance between the two of you, and you supersede the verbal. It's something kink people talk about a lot, and it can sound controversial to people who don't play like this, but the consent cues we read from each other are not limited to spoken words. Frederik would have known if a face slap was not OK, and the reason he knew that it was OK was because, after all these hours together, everything was in harmony. If it hadn't been, we both would have known, and we both would have stopped. This is completely different to when you start out – or, indeed, outside of a kink scenario, when you one hundred per cent need an unequivocal language-based consent for any kind of touch. And even when you have that, verbal consent is not enough if the physical cues disagree with the words.

Humans communicate far more with their bodies than their voices. It's much harder to lie with your body. I have seen people say, 'Yes, sure, that sounds great,' when their body language is clearly saying, 'Get away from me right now.' That is definitely *not* consent. The same is true in day-to-day life. 'No, I'm not upset,' you hear, from someone physically shaking with rage. 'Have a great day,' says the barista, while their hunched shoulders shout, 'You put milk in a single-origin, you total imbecile!' If we want real connection, we all need to pay attention to more than the words we say to each other.

Frederik could clearly see the effect the slap had had on me. He slapped and squeezed my face and throat more, and I begged to be allowed to come. He said he would count down from ten, and then I *had* to come. I loved the way he made my orgasms belong to him; they were at his command and under his control. And of course, I did as he said.

When I had finished shuddering and trembling, he asked if I could come again. I nodded.

'You come very easily!'

I said that yes, it was quite easy really, when I had been put in such a crazy state of arousal by all the beating, and the entire situation of flying to Norway just to put myself at his mercy all night.

'OK, make yourself come with your arse facing me.'

I turned around and he spanked me. Then he put one foot on my neck and face and one on my arse, and held me down with his legs as he watched me come. Next, he rested both feet on my back as if I was a footstool, and started caning me.

'My legs had better not fall off my footstool,' he warned.

I tried to stay still, but every stroke made me writhe.

Eventually, he decided it was time to go upstairs. I was not sure if this was for more torture, as he said he was bringing the dreaded loopy johnny with us. But I think he decided I had taken a lot; he said as much, and I was, of course, extremely proud. I thought I had been pathetic because I hadn't stayed in position, and had been unable to fully withstand everything he was so generously offering me. I had no way of comparing myself to others, but he kindly said I was on the upper end of the spectrum of what people can tolerate.

We talked about this a little. I'm always wary of asking about other subs, because it sounds like I want to be compared favourably and am fishing for compliments – it feels a little bit bratty. Some subs are self-defined 'brats' (lots of them love #kinktok!), and they and the doms they play with get off on it: being told to do something and then *not* doing it, being 'naughty'. It isn't my thing because it feels like the opposite of surrender, and I don't connect to the little girl/Daddy narrative. Anthony once said it doesn't work for him because if a sub says, 'No, not doing it,' with a bratty pout, he just thinks, *Cool, you don't have to*, and the whole play ends. Max says it just reminds him too much of the most irritatingly 'princesssy' women he's come across in real life – though there is no reason to think brats would have that personality outside of kink. As ever, it's easy to be dismissive of the kinks that don't happen to work for you, so I hope all the brats out there are having the best time, and that they get all the metaphorical ponies they ask for.

I also try not to ask about partners' other subs too much as I'm aware that even if they remain unnamed, they may not have given permission for their story to be told in any kind of detail. But it's fascinating how similar yet different things are between a different combination of people; the experiences we build together are unique between us. Anthony once described feeling that one sub of his was always halfway out of the room – he was never entirely sure she wasn't about to call it any second, and he would be very careful to ensure she really was happy right where she was. She never did leave, and she kept coming back for more, so presumably for her, the being on the edge of doubt was part of it, but he contrasted it to my general mentality of, *If I'm here, I am fully here, possibly for the next three days*, which is apparently evident in every pore. For him as a dom, this was very different. For me, being entirely present and committed to the moment is what makes the experience so rewarding and keeps me happy for weeks to come. Others get something completely different from it, and that is the excellent joy of human variety.

We went upstairs, and Frederik asked if I wanted to sleep in his bed, saying I deserved this because I had been brave. Of course I said yes, if that was OK. It was freezing, so I put on a T-shirt.

'Oh, no, no, no – you stay naked!' Frederik laughed.

We got into bed. I was wired but exhausted too, and was definitely ready to lie down. He kissed me quite chastely on the lips, but said we could hug if I wanted. I lay in his arms and felt a bit calmer.

I rolled over, thinking I would go to sleep on my side, nestling into a spooning position. Unfortunately, my arse pressing against his thigh just made the skin throb again, which woke me up and turned me on. After a little while of both of us clearly not sleeping, he began to tweak my nipple and grab my breasts. He guided my hand down to my cunt. I found it wetter than ever, and I began to moan. Then he pulled me over and pushed my head down to his cock. I hadn't even been sure if he was sleeping naked, and certainly would not have touched him uninvited. But he was clearly hard, and even in the dark, I could feel that his cock was . . . in proportion to the rest of him. I put my lips around it and realised that this was actually a bit of a challenge. Suddenly, I wished I was leaning backwards over something so my throat could open up and he could push in as deeply as he might want to.

Pulling me up and making me touch myself again, he switched on the light to watch, and again started to choke me and squeeze my face. I came really hard.

'You know, I still haven't punished you for forgetting your heels. That will happen in the morning.'

I have never heard a sentence less conducive to sleep.

❧

Our bodies have so many fascinating systems; the nervous system and the endocrine system and the interplay between them is beautiful. In the last decade, we've got so used to talking about the 'fight or flight' response as a negative, an ancient, antiquated system we should upgrade, because we no longer need that adrenaline; today, our stress tends to come in the form of 'I've got too many emails', rather than 'I'm being chased by a lion'. Modern anxiety seems to be all about this system kicking in when it shouldn't – and severe anxiety disorders and panic attacks sound absolutely devastating.

But the sympathetic nervous system can be a lot of fun, too. Apparently, when we perceive something as stressful or scary, the amygdala fires up and tells the hypothalamus to alert the adrenal glands. According to the Harvard University website, this is what happens next:

> *As epinephrine (also known as adrenaline) circulates through the body, it brings on a number of physiological changes. The heart beats faster than normal, pushing blood to the muscles, heart, and other vital organs. Pulse rate and blood pressure go up. The person undergoing*

> *these changes also starts to breathe more rapidly. Small airways in the lungs open wide. This way, the lungs can take in as much oxygen as possible with each breath. Extra oxygen is sent to the brain, increasing alertness. Sight, hearing, and other senses become sharper. Meanwhile, epinephrine triggers the release of blood sugar (glucose) and fats from temporary storage sites in the body. These nutrients flood into the bloodstream, supplying energy to all parts of the body.*[1]

Doesn't that sound . . . absolutely great?

One of the brilliant things for me about submission is triggering this response in my body, almost tricking it – which is why a situation has to feel real enough, otherwise my amygdala will be like, *Nah, definitely not a real lion, no adrenaline for you.* I want those heightened senses, that extra oxygen and that racing pulse when I'm with another person or people, as it will make every slap or stroke even more intense. And I am not alone, of course – the slightly unpleasant term 'adrenaline junkie' is a phrase for a reason.

Playing with the sympathetic nervous system can be fun, but experiencing real fear, in genuinely risky situations – not so much. There's nothing sexy about having to hold your keys in your hand as you walk down a canal towpath at dusk. You would think that as we get older, we would become more adept at being able to distinguish between the two, able to identify which racing pulse is caused by a harmless spider, and which is because

1 https://www.health.harvard.edu/staying-healthy/understanding-the-stress-response.

the building is actually on fire, but often it feels like we become so increasingly risk averse as we get more responsibilities in our lives, that we forget how fun adrenaline can be. In sport, you mitigate physical risk through competence; for me, diving off an eight-metre-high platform would be a genuinely life-threatening thing to do, but it is not dangerous for Tom Daley because his physical skills and training protect him. In *Free Solo*, Alex Honnold, with quite endearing arrogance, tries to explain how for *him*, climbing the awe-inspiring El Capitan rockface with no ropes or safety equipment whatsoever isn't as risky as it seems, because he is such an amazing climber.

As we learn more about ourselves and get better at communication – which comes gradually and with practice, like everything – I think situations that on paper might sound genuinely risky to people who haven't practised them, can feel much less risky for those who have. If you feel confident that you will be able to say clearly if you're uncomfortable or not enjoying something, or just feel like going home, flying to Oslo to visit a dom's house and be whipped all night is less daunting. Of course, Max knew where I was, I made sure my phone was charged, and I was sharing my location. I felt like I could easily have left and gone to a hotel if I had wanted to, but it seemed so unlikely; our first encounter and the messages we had exchanged had made me trust Frederik, and I could see that he was a kind and intelligent man – as well as one who was adept at activating all my arousing physical and mental pathways around humiliation and pain.

Zachary Zane, the excellent sex-positive influencer, talks about 'tolerance of risk'. He believes he is prepared to tolerate more risk in sex because, for him, the benefits far outweigh the risks. He seems to mostly be talking about STIs. I don't consider STIs particularly risky for me, as condoms are incredibly effective, and everyone I play with gets tested all the time – I love getting those 'Check out how clean I am . . . wanna play?' texts from kink friends. Showing off about your test results and bragging that you get tested – bring it on! Maybe one day we'll all have stickers, like the ones for when you got your Covid vaccine or you give blood. Personally, I don't think I am 'tolerating risk' more than anyone conventionally dating, as I think kink spaces are very safety conscious in all respects, but I *am* playing with my mind and body's fear systems, because I have found a safe space in which to do so.

❧

The next morning, the alarm went off too soon, and I briefly wondered where I was. I had a shower, the water stinging my destroyed skin. Frederik told me not to put on any tights or trousers. We went downstairs.

'Coffee, or punishment?'

I asked for punishment; I wouldn't be able to relax over a coffee if I was wondering what to expect. I had butterflies in my stomach.

He picked up the cane and told me to lie face down, flat on the floor. 'Lift up your foot.'

I misunderstood and raised my arse.

'No, your foot. It is important the punishment fits the crime.'

Now I understood. I bent one knee and offered him the sole of my foot, and my heart started beating quadruple time. He brought the cane down on the sensitive sole, and the sound was so loud for such a small area. I screamed into the rug.

'Just three on each foot. You can do that.'

And I managed to, offering the second foot when the time came.

Afterwards, Frederik made delicious Italian espressos, and we sat at the dining table, my feet tingling. It was nearly time to leave for my plane, so he inscribed *Spanking the Maid* for me:

Upwards toward the sky, girl.
You're getting better at it already.

He dropped me off at the airport, both of us smiling every time we passed a lorry. We had a nice talk in the car, happily discussing how nice it was to find a partner who tessellated so well with our own desires. We talked about how it's not only the specifics. Really, I can't say I like being caned in general. In fact, I have only ever wanted it and enjoyed it from two people, and the occasional other under Anthony's supervision. Frederik cannot say he wants to cane the soles of a woman's feet in general; it was just what felt right with me at the time, due to millions of tiny signals and where our time together had taken us.

We start from a basic position of 'I am a dominant and you are a submissive,' but exactly where that goes has infinite beautiful possibilities. It's why you can't plan every single thing in advance; it just doesn't work like that. My style of surrender worked with his style of dominance, and with what we were both in the mood for that chilly December. Our personalities also fitted together more generally. I am far more likely to find a connection in play with someone who shares some of my interests, and with whom I can have a really thoughtful conversation on the car ride home – especially if they also give me books.

Frederik asked me if I thought of S&M as a game. I replied truthfully that I do not. I have to feel that it is real, even though I know it isn't, otherwise it would feel silly, like a *Carry On* film. It has to involve actual fear, actual pain, actual surrender, actual trust. He said he thought I would say that, and that was his feeling too.

I have had other encounters where something jarred and it didn't quite work. When a dom seems needy, this upsets the balance for me – there is, perhaps strangely, a fine line between demanding and needy. Someone insisting, 'I need to see this photo from you NOW,' seems to put me in a position of power, which doesn't feel arousing. Similarly, physical criticism play doesn't do it for me. I remember one dom kept saying my tits were disgusting and looked like udders, and wanted me to list all the things I disliked about my body. I immediately thought, *Fuck right off*, and told him so. But I am sure that kind of play works well for some, and might even be a therapeutic approach to the body dysmorphia almost all women have. But you learn a lot from what doesn't work, too – despite my strong dislike for criticism of women's bodies in general, which I find hard to escape from even in role play, I really like the narrative of 'Your beauty will be overcome,' and the idea that just because a dom thinks I am hot, this does not mean I will not be bruised and bloodied, messy and tear-stained. This is the idea that beauty doesn't belong on a pedestal, that true beauty is not physical, and that my fully surrendered self is the most beautiful version of me. If they don't say I am hot in the first place, that story won't work. When I told Max this theory, he burst out laughing and said I just want everyone to tell me I'm pretty. Quite possibly!

I also don't enjoy it when people go too quickly into the pain without enough drama and scene-setting: the kind of 'Hello, bend over, here's a flogger' approach. That said, I am usually more than fine with, 'Hello, bend over, here's my cock.' For me, getting into a sexual headspace is easier and quicker than getting to the place where I can really enjoy pain. Learning all this is endlessly interesting to me, and contrasting it with what works for others is even more so. I am never upset with people with whom it didn't work – it's not that they've done something wrong, it's just that we didn't connect in that way.

Frederik and I hugged goodbye, and I wished I could convey more clearly how very grateful and happy I was for his . . . hospitality.

Walking through the airport, the soles of my feet stung, making it impossible not to relive every moment. On the plane, I read *Spanking the Maid* – much to the delight of the elderly man ordering red wine for breakfast in the seat next to me, who seemed to be reading it over my shoulder. It is an excellent book.

As time went on, Max and I went to fewer public parties and met fewer new dates from the internet. Instead, we spent more time with the people we had come to know and trust.

I love the life-affirming joy of connecting with someone new, or meeting a wonderful kinky stranger in a random situation – and the possibility of that happening really gets me out of bed in the morning. But I was finding that something possibly even more magical was happening through building trust with people over multiple sessions. After years and years, the places we could go to became wilder, and new horizons of strange beauty opened up. Together, after time, our imaginations could fuse. There was no anxiety and worry about meeting up in general, as there can be on first dates when you don't yet know how well you will gel or what the other person is into. I also found that, from my submissive point of view, new partners usually don't want to push you too far – although by date two, at least in Frederik's case, that did not seem to be a problem. Once you know someone well, I was discovering, there can be real, deliberately transcendental fear . . . and much more besides. The experience was moving beyond mind and body. I began to think of it in terms of soul.

Soul

Most people have, at some point experienced the sublime. There are myriad ways to describe that feeling: the sense of being connected to something bigger, of pure presence. Beyond happy or sad. The awe-inspiring feeling of being small in an infinite universe. Feeling the energy of all living things. Feeling the vastness of time. Our day-to-day concerns recede and become distant and petty. We realise, however fleetingly, what it's all about.

It comes to us all in so many different ways. Prayer, worship, meditation. Surfing in the powerful ocean, scaling a craggy mountain. Touching a tree. Running a marathon. Dancing in a club. Listening to music. Looking at a painting. Holding your baby for the first time. Holding the hand of your parent for what might be the last time. Humanity's long love affair with all drugs seems like it might be trying to find a shortcut to this place.

Professor David Nutt, the outspoken neuroscientist, compared brain imagery of people on the hallucinogen psilocybin against a fellow academic's studies of the brains of Tibetan monks during meditation. The images were very similar. In both cases, some systems of the brain were switched off, and without that noise, the participants felt transcendent. Professor Nutt, ever practical, said that this was all very well, but you can't send a PTSD patient to a monastery to train in meditation for forty-five years, and so he would stick to the chemical medical research, thanks.

If we're not seeking this feeling as a medical necessity, though, I wonder if having to work for it makes it more rewarding. That blissful runners' high does not come the first time you put on a pair of trainers. I wonder whether Damascene religious conversions really are always lightning-bolt moments, or if they are sometimes a product of gradual practice and prayer. Even with the shortcut of drugs, 'psychonauts' report their psychedelic experiences becoming better and better, as their brains and bodies find this plane more easily.

Whether you think of the feeling as divine, or as being caused by a particular combination of brain chemicals – or both – it seems that for everyone, these moments are the most important, the most meaningful, and make them feel most alive.

As time went on, I realised that more and more what I was seeking – and finding – in kink and sex was this kind of experience. The intellectual curiosity, discovery and learning, the growing confidence and trust, the delight in focusing on the body and the appreciation for what it can do – this was somehow giving way to an even richer sort of experience. With partners who had become regular over many years, I found we could push the boundaries further and further, trying different or more dramatic scenarios or techniques, unlocking new levels of feeling in our brains and bodies. But I also found that playing with strangers became more rewarding, too; Max and I both seemed to find people we connected with more easily, maybe because we were clearer about what we were looking for, and maybe because we were just more relaxed, educated and open-minded. I had learned that even things I would never have thought of trying might turn out to be fun, and was more chilled about giving them a go. I was amazed by how many coincidences there seemed to be; why did we keep meeting kinky people who were a great fit for us in the most random of circumstances? I began to believe we must be putting out some kind of kinky radar signal, or had tapped into a universal energetic field science had not yet discovered.

What had begun as an exciting investigation into a new world had developed into a fundamental facet of our relationship. While months could still go by when we did nothing kinky with anyone else, Max and I knew that it was always there, a reassuring undercurrent of possibility.

I cannot imagine living any other way.

For We Are Perverts and We Are Proud

In loving, proudly perverted, memory of Tobias

When Max and I discovered Kinky Salon, it changed our lives for ever. Kinky Salon London (KSL) was unlike any other night or party. If you have seen the film *Shortbus*, that's the closest cultural reference point, and even that doesn't begin to do it justice. Part immersive theatre, part cabaret, part festival, part full-on orgiastic sex party, it showed humanity at its most beautiful and made you happy to be alive.

A couple of times a year, KSL would host an event in different locations. There would be a theme, with a pun in the title and a dress code to match. There was *Plum Like It Hot*, where you had to dress as a fruit with a film-related twist. Another favourite was *Kinky Salon Mounts Olympus*. The idea here was Grecian gods and goddesses, but Max and I decided to go as sixties-style Olympic athletes. We thought this would be hilarious but everyone kept saying, 'Wait, are you the 118 guys? We don't get it. . .'. At Christmastime there was *Winter Is Cumming* and *Ride My Icicle*, and on other occasions we had a Roaring Twenties-themed *The Great Twatsby* and a comic book-themed *Cartoon Strip*.

Rather than fetishwear, we were encouraged to go in creative fancy dress related to the theme. Some people had staggeringly amazing outfits that looked like what would happen if Guillermo del Toro's costume designer ran away to join the circus. Max and I always looked more like we were wearing *Blue Peter* projects. One Christmas, we went as a Nativity sheep and a shepherd; I stitched a random bit of brown suede together for Max's jerkin, and wrapped myself as artfully as possibly in a fake sheepskin rug from IKEA. The jerkin got reused for *Kinky Salon Does Panto*, when Max came as the woodcutter, and I an ironically virginal, corset-clad Snow White.

It was the era of the Kigu: Japanese animal onesies that had a bizarre moment in London. It was not unusual to see a felt crocodile walking through London Fields early in the morning, or a human-sized monkey dancing on a roof terrace. I wore a tiger one when we went as Calvin and Hobbes for *Cartoon Strip*, and we had matching penguin ones for a winter theme. They were very easy to slip out of, which was necessary to do early on, as they were made of an incredibly sweaty polyester fleece.

On arriving at KSL, you waited in a holding area before being ushered into an antechamber in groups of about eight. You would be welcomed by a fawn, or an Elizabethan bard, or an alien or a dragon, who would then explain the proceedings and elicit agreement from participants to the Kinky Salon Charter. Although performed theatrically, the charter was a serious and detailed set of extremely sensible rules about consent, privacy, inclusivity, and not being a dickhead.

When this intro was complete, the curtains would swing open, and I would often get tears in my eyes at the extreme level of dedication the – largely volunteer – crew had gone to in creating a secret world. The sets were amazing, and there were always so many weird and wonderful things to see and do. For the first couple of hours, we would run around looking at everything, getting invited to play strange games by mysterious figures, or being beckoned into hidden doorways.

At 11 p.m., there would be a kind of summoning, and everyone would gather on the main dancefloor, where we'd be told to sit down on the floor. People would get tangled in each other's elaborate costumes, and surveying the scene, it was easy to think, *What strange film am I an extra in right now?*

Then there would be a cabaret. The acts were always completely bananas, from bawdy burlesque to sexy magicians, with circus performers, dancers, music and poetry. Sometimes the performers were very famous; sometimes they were KSL participants who had asked for a spot to try something new.

At the end of the cabaret, we were all invited to make the Kinky Salon Pledge. It was call and response, and went like this:

MC: Place your right hand on your heart.
(We all did.)
MC: Place your left hand on your neighbour's buttock.
(We all asked if that was fine by our neighbour, and if so, did that.)
MC: Now repeat after me: In Pervitude and Servitude—
Us: IN PERVITUDE AND SERVITUDE—
MC: United by our dubious morals—
Us: UNITED BY OUR DUBIOUS MORALS—
MC: Well dressed and ready for action—
Us: WELL DRESSED AND READY FOR ACTION!
MC: Call us perverts, for we are proud.
(With a fist in the air.)
Us: CALL US PERVERTS FOR WE ARE PROUD!
(With a roar of excitement.)

And with that, the rest of the night began.

New spaces would now be opened: the playrooms, where gigantic sex spaces had been created by joining masses of king-sized beds together. There was sometimes a dungeon area with intriguing pieces of equipment too. These spaces were always separated from the main rooms by curtains. A DJ would start playing, and the main space would become a dancefloor. Bars would open and other random things, maybe a coconut shy or a tarot reader.

Once, Max and I were determined to be the first people exhibitionistically fucking in the very middle of the playroom. We dashed in, threw off our costumes, and leapt upon each other. Soon, a man and a woman approached us. They were naked, having already discarded their outfits, and asked if they could join in. They had a vehemently positive response from us. Max was fucking me from behind, and the man moved to my head and lifted his cock to my lips. The woman kissed him for a bit, watching him fuck my mouth, before moving round to Max. We spent the next hour in various combinations with them, as the beds filled up around us. When we decided it was time for a break, we had to climb our way out through a mass of sweaty, writhing limbs.

Other times, we would spend time round the venue catching up with old friends and making new ones. If the DJs were great, we would dance. There was no pressure to head to the playrooms, and you didn't feel like you weren't participating in the night if you chose not to.

The dancefloor would often have a certain population of naked, post-play inhabitants – I was sometimes among them, only because I couldn't relocate my costume underneath the sea of bodies.

We would be dancing or chatting with new people, and someone might say, 'Would you like to head to the playroom?' If we all did, we'd skip inside and try to find a limb-free corner. If you asked someone and they said they didn't feel like it, it didn't feel like a huge rejection. More like if you offered to buy them a drink and they said, 'Not right now, thanks.'

KSL was the most inclusive party I have ever been to. No gender or sexuality was preferred above another.

It was racially diverse and international – you would hear different languages being spoken, as people would travel from throughout Europe, or further, to attend. There were bodies of every shape and size; the silly fancy dress was much more of a leveller than 'sexy' clothes or latex ever are. We met wheelchair users there, and once Max found someone's prosthetic limb in the playroom and waved it aloft, concerned its owner might have misplaced it. In fact, on one occasion, Max had broken his leg and was in a cast and on crutches, but was determined not to miss the event. As I recall, he got quite a lot of attention that night . . .

We made friends at KSL who have gone on to become extremely important people in our lives, both in and out of the bedroom. It was the kind of place that made intimacy easy. There was a childlike innocence to proceedings that made you feel like you were normal, even if you were dressed as an aubergine and being asked if you liked pegging.

Sadly, KSL is no more. In London, licensing is going backwards, and I think it's harder than ever to create imaginative, protected spaces of this sort today.

I don't believe in a heaven, apart from the ones we can create for ourselves on earth, but if I did, it would look a lot like Kinky Salon.

Once, when Max and I hooked up with a cute couple we met online, we all went for a drink together and the conversation turned to fear of rejection. They were saying that they had noticed since they had been CNM (consensually non-monogamous) and meeting people in the kink world, they had both begun to overcome their deeply ingrained fears of rejection. Max and I agreed; we felt the same.

I think a lot of our social fear comes from that *Will they like me?* feeling that most of us seem to pick up in the school playground, if not before, and then have reinforced throughout our lives. Little girls especially are taught to people-please before they can even crawl; it's hard not to see any kind of rejection as a massive failure when pleasing others is so deeply ingrained. I have been on so many exploratory dates to meet kink people where the text afterwards has come back saying: 'Lovely to meet you, but no thanks.' You learn not to take it personally, because there are so many reasons the person or people might not be into it: your fetishes might not match, a couple might decide against pursuing CNM in general, or other commitments might have taken precedence – somehow, it's easier to see that they might just not be into *it* rather than *you*. If you go to a party and you don't find anyone you want to play with, or who wants to play with you, it's still a fun night. It's so different to the monogamous marriage-and-kids-orientated dating game, where every meeting is charged with such pressure. No wonder we are all terrified of rejection when we play it. I am far more likely to spend sleepless nights worried about having offended a 'normal' friend, or to experience social anxiety about attending a work dinner or family wedding, than I am to feel upset about being turned down by someone I approach within a kink context. I don't know them, I never have to see them again. It's easier for me to feel 'easy come, easy go' about it. Literally . . .

I once shared this theory with Anthony, and he agreed. He said he would obviously never for a second feel offended if he suggested caning to a model and she said absolutely not, and he had come to realise that this was no different to someone just turning you down for anything else. If they don't like caning, it's not about you, but if they don't want to go for a coffee, that's not about you either.

This is one of the ways in which it feels to me that kink people have sometimes 'done the work', as therapists say. If you have a lot of interactions, and so necessarily a lot of rejections, you are going to get better at it. Much later, I heard of 'rejection therapy', where people practise experiencing rejection, usually by approaching strangers in contexts where they wouldn't normally. The idea seems to be that you get used to people thinking you are crazy, but that you also begin to care less. In addition, you will be surprised by how many people do not reject you. Spend a month on any CNM or kink app, and you will get the same emotional lessons (and probably have much more fun than you would going up to people in the supermarket).

❧

It was my favourite kind of sticky, humid, New York evening. I was having dinner with an old friend on a sidewalk table in the West Village.

After dinner, he mentioned he was invited to the launch of a new music magazine. It was the kind of sultry night of possibility where you don't say no to parties. We went along. It was in a trendy warehouse loft space. We ambled around, and my friend introduced me to people. In the queue for the toilet, I chatted to a nice guy who said the party was dying and he was going to have an afterparty in his apartment, if I wanted to join. Again, I blame the you-can't-say-no weather for my hearty acceptance.

Twenty or so people ended up at the afterparty, somewhere down in Chinatown. I started talking to a man called Abe. He was really interesting, clearly very clever, and had a genuinely *good* job actually making a difference in the world. Also, I decided, he was really hot. I was enjoying talking to him so much, but a great track came on and I really needed to dance. My boots seemed to be hampering this, but they had so very many buckles. I sat down on the floor to undo them, Abe laughing at me. Finally I was free and barefoot, and started jumping around. Others joined in, and Abe took my hand and started twirling me around, first by my hand, and then with his arm circled around my waist. *Huh*, I thought. *Are you suggesting something?*

After some particularly high-spirited dancing, he leaned in and we kissed. My whole body reacted. *This*, I thought, *is what humid late nights are for.*

It turned out he was staying in the apartment we were in with his friend; he lived in Austin and was visiting. He asked me where I was staying, and I told him my apartment was in Brooklyn.

He looked at me. 'You wanna get out of here?'

I liked him – he was clever and hot and fun – but it was late, and what, really, are the chances of a random one-night stand being anything to write home about? Was I just considering this because I associated this kind of sticky evening with sex, and because I was horny? Max was in London and I didn't have any current NYC partners, and I couldn't really be bothered with using apps to find one.

'I'm not sure,' I said.

He shrugged and grinned, and started dancing with me once more. This made me want to kiss him again, and as I did so, he took my chin firmly. In that microsecond, I felt a different kind of touch. Our eyes met.

'Sooooo – Uber?' I said.

In the cab, all bets were off. As we crossed the bridge, he had one hand around my throat, choking me, while the other was thrusting into my cunt. He was whispering all the things he was going to do to me, and I could only respond in kind. I was so delighted that a surprise party hook-up seemed to be turning . . . well, kinky. I would have had *no* idea.

We tumbled into my apartment. He had a way of touching me that made me know instantly that he could do whatever he wanted to my body and I would be helpless – and I would love it. He tweaked my nipples *hard*, he slapped my face, he ordered me onto my knees, and I knew he could see how much all of this was turning me on, which was encouraging him to up the ante. I could see how much my submissive sluttiness was working for him, so I went more and more into the fantasies.

I love a talker – when you say, 'And then I would beg you to fuck my holes,' and they come back with, 'Oh, you will have no choice, you'll be tied up and I will rip all three apart, and then my friends will come and fuck your disgusting stretched cunt, and we will all come on your face . . .' – it's great.

Within about twenty minutes, he had been inside me, brutally, everywhere possible, and I think he was beginning to see it might not all be just talk with me. He came on my face, then, somehow, he pulled me out of the apartment and back onto the street. He had put his clothes back on, but I was naked. He made me face the wall and spread my legs. An early-morning jogger ran past and pretended not to look. It must have been about 5 a.m. He had my phone in his hand, and started filming me as he asked me to touch myself, in view of the street. I thought it was quite gentlemanly of him to use my phone, not his – it was about the humiliation in the moment, not him trying to record for his own use, and maybe he wanted to me to feel safe about that. Or perhaps my phone had just been nearer. Of course, he had no idea that the internet is littered with pictures of me doing far worse, so I was unlikely to mind if a lovely-seeming man kept some erotic souvenirs of a fun night.

Back inside, we got some wine. He sat on the sofa, and I straddled him.

'Tell me a story. I can tell you are a whore, and I know you have stories. Tell me a real one.'

The great thing about having spent a lot of time writing up lots of my more outlandish encounters in my diary, and rereading them pretty often, was that they were quite present in my mind. I thought for a moment, then looked him in the eyes and told him about a time when I had met a hot guy on the plane to New York. We landed, and then a few hours later I went round to the Standard and he fucked me in view of the High Line, pressed up against those glass windows. When I left, I went straight round the corner to another guy's hotel, and then came home covered with both their cum.

I could feel his hardening cock under my cunt as I spoke, which was making me writhe around, wanting it inside me.

'Uh uh. Not yet. I need more stories. Tell me one from when you were young.'

I considered this, and then told a story that was, in my opinion, quite sweet, about having a crush on my English teacher and losing my virginity to his son, who was in my year at school. I'm not sure Abe thought it was sweet.

'I bet you want to be pissed on, don't you? Tell me a story about that.'

One anecdote sprang to mind, and by the end of my recounting of a particularly urine-filled night, we were fucking again, him holding my hips in a strong grip and grinding me onto his cock.

He pulled out, and I thought he would flip me over, but instead he pulled me and pushed me into the bathroom.

'Get in there.' He pointed.

I knew what he wanted. I knelt down in the bath, tipped my head back and opened my mouth wide.

'Oh, you have to beg me. This is for you, not me.'

I begged, and a stream of hot piss shot into my mouth and over my face.

Abe had to go back to Austin to catch a flight, so reluctantly we called it a night. We exchanged numbers, and within about five minutes of him leaving, we were texting each other: 'What the FUCK just happened?'

I had a shower and got into bed, far too wired to sleep, mulling on how quickly a 'vanilla' party flirtation had gone full kink in record-breaking time. We were both equally to blame – responding and escalating as we each grew more confident that the other wasn't going to freak out.

In the months that followed, the level of long-distance WhatsApp-based filthiness with Abe was unrelenting. He liked me to squat over my phone camera, spreading my cunt and arse so he could see, while I told him stories. Ideally, he liked me to do this in a public bathroom when I was out for dinner. A particular favourite story of ours involved me going to a farmyard and being fucked by all the animals in order, ending with a gigantic horse. I was so happy to have chance-met a person who was there for such wholesome vignettes.

I am genuinely not sure if I am somehow drawn to doms, and they to me, when I come across them in real life. Perhaps there is some kind of cellular instinct: a 'domdar', as Max has taken to calling it. Or maybe it is actually just such an incredibly common type of fantasy (let's revisit that stat – ninety-six per cent of women and ninety-three per cent of men!) that it is more to do with giving permission and making each other feel comfortable enough that we won't be ridiculed or pathologised.

I am better now at communicating my desires, even on a first meeting – both verbally and physically – and maybe that means I 'meet' more doms. Really, I think it's just that I give people a safe-seeming space in which to reveal themselves, and vice versa. I have no doubt that a week later, Abe could have hooked up with a less-deranged pervert, or at least someone who was not coming across like that, and could have enjoyed some equally hot sex that featured zero gang-bang and bestiality fantasising. And if he had turned out to be more of a sub, I know we would have had a great time anyway, just maybe not playing with the BDSM fantasies. Or I might have switched, just for the hell of it! As ever, the magic lies in the communion of our desires and the way our fantasies fuse in their own unique, fun way.

❧

As the years passed and my relationships with some doms deepened, I noticed a new element seeping into play. I began to find a feeling of devotion, even worship. This was different to surrender and submission. It felt more active, like something more than only giving my body and surrendering control. This developed slowly, over time. It felt real and natural. The thought followed the experience, not the other way around.

I was reminded of the tradition of courtly love in medieval poetry. The whole concept is extremely kink. There is an elaborate, codified role play of how a courtly knight should behave towards the female object of his devotion. There is nothing more noble than to sacrifice your life for your love. In *The Meaning of Courtly Love*, scholar Francis Newman describes it as 'a love at once illicit and morally elevating, passionate and disciplined, humiliating and exalting, human and transcendent'. I can relate.

The concept can be linked to extreme fetish. in *Le Roman de la Rose*, one of the most iconic medieval poems about courtly love, entire pages are devoted to the description and worship of a rose. This serves as an allegory for the object of his affection, but is so reminiscent of the way some people are intrinsically aroused by particular objects.

The devotional language of religion and spiritual worship was co-opted in these poems for romantic love – and, indeed, it seemed that to love in this way, in the context of the poems, was sublime, and brought you closer to God. The way you loved, mimicking the way you worshipped Christ, would elevate you from a worldly to a spiritual plane. (However, as Lancelot finds at the hands of Malory and other less romantic writers, you can't get carried away and think of romantic love as being *above* Christian devotion – no Holy Grail for you if so.)

In a modern, secular world, do we lack this experience of devotion? Few of us would want it in our romantic partnerships or platonic friendships. Today, we tend to want equality, trust, empathy, support and a healthy attachment style, rather than someone who is willing to go out and get run through with a lance on our behalf. If we do not worship a deity or have a special devotional practice of any kind, when do we get to feel this millennia-old human feeling?

One day, I went to see Anthony. As usual, he told me to hang my dress on the pegs in the hall and come upstairs to the 'parlour' naked except for my shoes. Immediately, he sat down on the sofa and took out his cock. He told me to kneel on the wooden floor in front of him and to suck it. I got overly enthusiastic and he reprimanded me. 'This is a not a sprint. You are going to be there for a long, long time. Relax. Think about what you are doing. Every tiny movement of your head and jaw and tongue.'

When you know something is going to be very long, you become more patient. When you think something is going to be short, like queuing at a checkout, and it turns out to be long, that's when you get bored and antsy, because you are not accepting the experience. I read long books more slowly than short ones; I know I am going to read them over weeks, not hours, so I don't race through them. It's nice when a book is with you for a while. Max tends to read epic tomes, sometimes over the course of a whole year; he will remember 2019 as the year of *The Three Musketeers*, or 2010 as the year of *A Brief History of Time*. Very little is inherently boring; it only becomes so if you are thinking about the next thing. I thought of minimalist composers like Philip Glass and Steve Reich, who use a pattern repeated again and again, to the point where you come through what seems like boring repetition to another plane; in listening to them, you have to accept that the joy is not going to come from being thrillingly entertained by new tunes and drama, but from giving in to the repetition.

I thought about all this, and I began to see kneeling before Anthony's cock as a devotional experience. Physically, I was the active one, as he was lying back, so it was different from when he caned me, for example. But as I began to accept that I had no idea how long I would be there, and that my whole purpose at this point was to bring him pleasure, for as long as he wanted, it felt sublime. If he got close to coming, he would slow me down or move me. I felt like the more I gave, the more I had to give, like Shakespeare's Juliet:

> My bounty is as boundless as the sea,
> My love as deep. The more I give to thee,
> The more I have, for both are infinite.

We were there for three hours.

It was trippy and such a different dynamic: a different kind of submission that could only have worked after all this time.

❧

I had been feeling palpitation-inducingly scared about seeing Francois again. He was such a surprise: so dark, and so unpredictable, and so very good-looking. When we first met, it had seemed like such a coincidence that he was an experienced dom.

My company had sent me to a pretty dull event to take notes on some new technology, which as far as I could see was entirely irrelevant to our business. As the presentation went on, my attention was waning, and I started gazing around the auditorium. My eyes met a similarly rebellious pair across the aisle. We smiled at each other, then looked dutifully back to the stage. Five minutes later, we looked at each other again. He mouthed, 'This is *boring*.' I nodded. He gestured his head to the exit. I laughed, shrugged and nodded again.

We crept outside, giggling like teenagers. We went for a drink and talked liked business professionals. By the third drink, we were properly flirting, and by the fourth, he had cancelled his flight to the States that evening and booked a hotel room. Somehow, emboldened by alcohol, the existence of said hotel room, and the fact we had discovered our businesses were entirely unrelated and we would never have to work together, the conversation turned to sexual preferences. Twelve years earlier, if someone had asked me about that on a first date, there is no way I would have said, as I did now, 'Well, sometimes I like to be tied up, choked, flogged, beaten and humiliated.' I was ready to make it a joke – 'Ha ha, got you!' – depending on his reaction. But almost immediately, his dark French eyes got deeper and darker. I quickly clarified, 'But only with people who know what they are doing, and who I can trust.'

He smiled. 'By chance, I do have a little experience in this field.'

What had followed was a night of untold chaotic, messy, sometimes hilarious, getting-to-know-you submission. He was extreme, and had no shame about his desires. Some of our kinks coincided, while to some of his I said, 'Absolutely no way in hell.' We had texted a bit after, but it didn't seem likely we would ever meet again.

Then, he announced that he would be attending a conference he knew I would be at. *Interesting*, I thought.

We started messaging at the beginning of the conference week. I would beg to be allowed to be his slave, and he would deny I was up to it, listing all the humiliating things I would have to do, and doubting my capabilities. He liked breath play, and would tell me about the plastic bag he would hold over my head. I knew he was water sports-obsessed, so I would tell him how I would beg to be pissed on. His vibe was very much: *You are such a slut, you will do anything degrading for me.* It's different to the pain-focused kind of submission, but for me it connects right back to my earliest Bible story fantasies – the Pharisees bringing the adulteress to Jesus to see what he would do with her. Jesus writes something in the sand; biblical scholars debate endlessly about what it said. As young as I was, I imagined myself as the adulteress, shamed and marched around the town, even when I didn't understand what her sin was. Later, when I did, I reconnected to that scene in my fantasies. My version of the adulteress was so slutty she couldn't help but give herself to all the men of the town, even though she knew what her humiliating punishment might be. The Pharisees had all fucked her, one after the other, seeing how wet she was, before they took her to be judged. When I read *The Scarlet Letter* at university, the contrast between writing serious essays about its meaning, history and the patriarchy, and the fact I was unable to resist wanking over the idea of myself being branded with a red 'A' later in the evening, made me feel full of shame and consternation about what a freak I must be. Now, with Francois, it was exactly this kind of feeling I was playing with. It felt like such a blessing to be able to do this, freely and joyfully, and remarkable to have, by chance, met someone I could do it with.

He was planning to stay in the main conference hotel for the one night he was coming. This was both convenient and rather risky in terms of a lack of subtlety.

I had been out to a dinner, and arrived in the hotel bar at around 11.30 p.m. It was thronged with people attending the big conference party. I battled through the crowd, saying hello to people I knew, but keenly looking out for Francois. Suddenly, I heard someone shout my name, and turned to find an industry acquaintance, Jake, gesturing for me to come over. Standing next to him was Francois.

'Sonnet, so good to see you. Would you like a drink? Let me get one for you. Do you know Francois?'

Francois looked down at me from his towering height and smiled a very cute smile. 'Yes, we met at our presentation in London.' He kissed me hello.

Jake said he would go to get us some drinks. He disappeared into the crowd, and Francois smirked down at me.

'Er . . . how was your day?' I asked.

Some people from my industry came over, and I introduced them; everyone kissed hello, everyone gossiped about work, everyone laughed. Francois was polite and charming and funny, which I found hilarious, as it was so unlike what I knew him for.

After a while, he told the group he should probably be going. He leaned in to me, and whispered, in a somehow menacing tone, 'Room 372, fifteen minutes.' I grinned in happiness. He glared at me, already playing.

I waited for a few minutes, then went out to the lobby. I looked round shadily to see if anyone would notice me getting into the lift. The coast seemed clear.

Once I was upstairs, I knocked on the door, praying I had remembered the correct number.

He shouted, 'Come in.'

I pushed open the door. It was a big suite, and Francois was lying on the bed in the middle, naked except for his pants. He had a beautiful body, but I knew immediately he was in character, and there wasn't going to be any polite chit-chat.

He beckoned me over, not smiling. 'So, you want to be my slave?'

I nodded.

'You understand that you have to do what I want, however humiliating?'

I nodded again.

'What? You can speak, can't you?'

'Yes,' I said.

'Good. And how does that make you feel? Are you getting wet just thinking about how I am going to treat you?'

I began to nod, but then remembered to speak. 'Yes.'

'Slut. Take off your clothes and put them on that chair, then come here and stand in front of me.'

I did so, and for a while he just looked at me, not speaking.

Then he slowly got up and towered above me. 'Count.' He then slapped my face over and over, while I counted. Unfortunately, I had stupidly accepted a line of coke earlier in the evening, and I think it had a numbing effect. He was going to keep on till I really broke down – there would be no faking anything with him. So it took a lot of slaps, and ended with me on my knees, tears falling down my cheeks.

Then he said, 'I need to piss.'

I'd known we would rapidly come to his urine fixation, so I was not at all surprised.

'You need to go into the bathroom and kneel down, with your mouth wide open; you are my toilet.'

I crawled into the luxurious bathroom, which had a large wet room-style shower area. I knelt down with my face lifted up, as directed.

He came in and without acknowledging me at all, pulled out his cock and pissed all over my face and into my mouth. It seemed to go on for ages, until I was completely covered and had swallowed a huge amount. Surprisingly, it was not disgusting, though it was certainly gross enough to be completely humiliating. I felt quite happy that in the course of our messages, he had asked whether I would ever be shat on, and I had responded very adamantly in the negative.

When he was done, he put on his pants.

'You can have one minute in the shower. Cold.'

He switched on the shower and an icy blast hit me. I screamed and tried to move back out. He pushed me back in with his foot, saying, 'You are disgusting and covered in piss; you need to be washed.'

It was so cold. Finally, he switched it off. I stood up gingerly. I knew I must look awful. My make-up was running, the water had failed to wash off much of the urine, and I was shivering.

'How do you feel?' he asked.

'Cold, humiliated, dirty,' I mumbled.

'Come here.' He grabbed my hair and pulled me towards him, then bent me over the sink and thrust his fingers into my cunt. 'So why is your pussy all dripping wet? Why, slut? You like being my toilet? I think you want to come. Should I let you? Is that a nice treat for my little slave?'

I said, 'Yes, please.'

He pulled me up and out of the bathroom and to the hotel room door, without letting me dry myself at all.

'OK, you are going to walk out into the corridor, then walk across the hall to the far wall. Slowly. Then you are going to come back, and kneel down a metre from my door.'

'But . . . no . . . I can't,' I weakly protested.

He put his fingers into my cunt again. 'Ha, you get wetter just at the thought of it. Slut.' He opened the door. 'Go.'

I was genuinely petrified, as almost everyone staying in the hotel was in my industry, including several senior colleagues. But I also thought that not doing what he said would involve a worse punishment, and I was engrossed enough in the role play that it was this I was more concerned about. So I walked out, completely naked, wet, covered in piss, with my make-up running down my red, slapped face. I walked as slowly as I could, and it felt like the longest walk I'd ever taken.

When I got to the far wall, he shouted, 'Stop.'

I stood, facing the wall. Seemingly hours passed, though I am sure it was just seconds.

'OK, you can come back now.'

I walked back towards his room, then paused a metre from his door and knelt down.

'Good. Now lie down and spread your legs,' he said from the doorway, looking down at me.

I did, leaving patches of water and piss all over the floor.

'Now, look up at me as you make yourself come.'

I started to touch my cunt, trying to block out the thought of anyone passing by and seeing me damp, messy, naked and lying in a hotel corridor, touching myself while observed disinterestedly by a nearly naked French telecoms millionaire. Annoyingly – and surprisingly for me – I couldn't come quickly. Then I remembered the line of coke! Enemy of orgasms whatever your gender, it is a terrible drug for sex, but one that people think will give them the faux confidence needed to pursue it. Any more than one line a few hours ago, and I should not have been there; I tend to take the view it's not fair on a good dom for you not to know your real limits and communicate them. And if you're not with a good person, you are making yourself very vulnerable in real life. If I want to be spanked, for example, but I am not brave enough to ask for it – or to accept it – without drugs, then I need to do some more work in my brain first. The shortcut won't get me there faster, and it won't be better.

'You know you are not coming in till you come, and if you fake it, I will know. But I am getting bored so come now,' he said.

Weirdly, the pressure of being told to come on cue was somehow outweighed by the general humiliation and being ordered around, and I did then come quickly, looking up at him as I did so.

I was about to get up when he suddenly closed his room door, leaving me lying outside in the corridor with my legs spread, alone.

He opened the door again. 'Do you need to piss?'

'Er, not really.'

'This is pathetic. I need you to come, and you can't. I need you to piss, and you can't.' He pulled me back inside and took me into the bathroom. 'I am going to need you to provide a lot of piss for me. I am going to need you to drink it, and to be covered in it. So you need to drink water now. Eight full glasses, quickly.'

It turns out downing eight glasses of water is very hard work. Especially if you're spanked very hard whenever you pause. Finally, I finished all eight.

He pulled me out into the bedroom. He lay down on the bed, and took off his pants. His cock was hard, and very big, as I remembered. He pulled me over him. I really needed to piss after all the water. I asked to go to the bathroom.

'No. You piss when I say. Since you have been a good slave up till now, you can suck my cock.'

'Thank you so much,' I said.

I straddled him, and leaned over and began to lick his cock. Then I put my lips around it and moved my head right down, nearly choking myself.

'Pull my balls,' he said, so I did.

'Now put your finger in my arse.' So I did that.

I could feel him nearly coming. Suddenly, he grabbed my hair with one hand and pulled my face up so it was an inch above his cock. With the other hand, he grabbed his cock, directing his warm stream of cum round my face.

'OK. You must need to piss now.' I really, really did. He went and got a glass from the cupboard. 'Piss into this and fill it up and bring it back. But leave the door open. And do not wash yourself.'

I went into the bathroom, and did as I was told. I came back with a big glass of urine. I stood in front of the bed.

'You are going to drink it all. Hand me the glass.'

I gave him the glass. He stood up. He stroked my fringe away from my face, and with one hand pulled my hair, forcing my head back. Then he told me to open my mouth. He lifted the glass of my urine to my mouth, and slowly tilted it in. He poured slowly and gradually, making sure I swallowed it. Then, when I had drunk half the glass, he suddenly tipped the whole glass up, so the liquid choked me and spilled out all over my lips and face and dribbled down my chin, mingling with his cum.

He put the glass down, and lay back down on the bed. He gestured for me to straddle him. I did. I could feel his cock underneath my cunt, but I knew much better than to try and put it inside me without being invited.

He leaned back with his hands behind his head.

'OK, close your eyes. If you ever open them, even slightly, even for a second, you are going out in the hallway. Each time you do it, you will go there for longer. But now we are going to talk. We can ask three questions each.'

I closed my eyes. This seemed oddly generous for his role and like a conversation. As if he knew what I was thinking, he slapped my face.

'Slave, this is not some kind of first date. I am rewarding you. But I go first. Have you ever been paid for sex?'

'Um, yes,' I said. (We'll come back to this later.)

'You are a prostitute too, then. I am not surprised. Tell me about it.'

I opened my eyes. Big mistake.

'What is wrong with you? Can you not follow a basic instruction? Get out there. Now.'

I walked out into the hall. I tried to leave the door on the latch.

'Close the door properly!' he shouted from the bed.

I stood outside, cold and wet and covered in his piss, my piss and his cum. It felt like an eternity.

Finally, he opened the door. 'OK. Now, don't do it again.' He pulled me inside, and quickly put his fingers up into my cunt, which was still very wet. He raised his eyebrows. We resumed our position on the bed. He held my hips so my cunt was pressed against his cock. I closed my eyes.

'So, you were telling me about how you are a prostitute. How many men have you fucked for money?'

'Umm . . . I think five,' I said.

'Do you like it?'

'Sometimes . . .'

'Well, I don't know why anyone would pay you, slut. OK, second question. What is your most disgusting secret fantasy?'

I nearly opened my eyes. It is so hard to talk to someone with your eyes closed, but it certainly had the desired effect of making me feel utterly vulnerable. Somehow, the fact that I *could* open my eyes, but wasn't allowed to, made it more effectively humiliating than a blindfold. I was *choosing* to submit. Doms have often said to me that this does it for them more than the force: making a sub stand still, of her own volition, when being flogged, rather than restraining her so she physically cannot move; telling her not to make a sound, but not gagging her. They say there is a sublime beauty in that kind of surrendered obedience. To be honest, both versions work well for me. Allowing myself to be restrained feels like one kind of surrender, and the more active experience of doing as I'm told even when it's hard to is another kind.

I thought about my darkest never-to-be-enacted fantasies. 'I suppose, being fucked by a dog.'

'I know that already, slut. We all know that. Remember I said I was going to walk you in the forest outside Paris? So what happens in your fantasy?'

I made up a story as I went about someone forcing me to live in a cage with their Alsatian . . . it was totally disgusting, but telling it tremblingly while straddling someone and being so dominated was hot. For me, fantasies that are strongly 'imagination only' are often about the telling; I love playing with the idea that I am being 'forced' to reveal how disgusting and filthy I am. It was only when I ceased to think that I was, in fact, disgusting forever having imagined that kind of thing, that I found I could play with it. In my teens and twenties, it was actual shame, not play shame. And that is not hot.

'I can feel your cunt getting my cock wet,' he said, forcing my hips down again.

My eyelids flickered.

'Careful. It's five minutes next time. Now, your third question. What would you like me to do to you – if you could have anything?'

I thought this was interesting . . . I couldn't actually think of anything more depraved, since I'd just essentially told him I wanted him to make a dog fuck me. So I said, I wanted him to fuck me – in a normal, vanilla way.

'Ha, I know you want my cock, and you can have it if I decide you are worth it. But as a slave, getting a gift. You want to open your eyes and look at me, don't you?'

I shook my head.

'Yeah, you do. But your turn. Ask me a question.'

I wondered if this was some strange mind game or simply his version of pillow talk.

'Um, OK. Do you have other slaves?'

'Yes.'

'What do they do for you?'

He started to tell me about a girl who he only sees with his dog, and he treats them the same, feeding them in adjacent bowls and walking them together, and they both sleep curled up on the foot of his bed. And even his actual girlfriend, who now has to go everywhere with increasingly heavy Chinese balls and no knickers. I wondered whether this was invented, like my Alsatian story, or true, or – more likely – a blurry mix of fantasy and reality, dramatised for the sake of our current reality. I had long since stopped assuming extreme stories were only that, as I had met so many weird and wonderful people blissfully living out their fetishes with willing participants.

'Next question.'

'Umm . . . so, how did you turn out like this?'

He lost his role for a second and let out a big belly laugh. 'So the slut prostitute covered in cum and piss, desperate for a guy she barely knows who makes her stand in a hotel corridor naked to fuck her, wants to know what *my* problem is?'

I burst into laughter and opened my eyes.

He quickly snapped out of it. 'Oh, slut, you are useless. Corridor.'

'Nooo, I don't want to . . .'

'Get out there now,' he said, slapping my face hard.

I went outside, closing the door. I looked around nervously, realising that all the people who'd stay up late would be coming out of the bar around now. I just hoped desperately that all the senior people had gone to bed already.

At last, the door opened and he pulled me back in, again, testing to see how wet my cunt was.

He sighed. 'You see, you act like this is horrible, but your pussy tells me the truth. I am only giving you what you want.'

We went back to the bed.

'Let's try again. I will tell you my story, but only if you keep your eyes closed, and don't writhe on my cock, getting it all wet.'

I nodded with my eyes tightly closed.

'So, when I was seventeen, I had a beautiful girlfriend. All my friends were jealous. She was twenty-five, and so gorgeous, and cool. One day, she broke up with me – I couldn't understand it. She gave all these excuses, but I didn't believe them. I kept pestering her for the truth. Finally, she told me. She said she was a submissive, that she could only be with someone who could make her live like a slave, and that she didn't think I could do that. I said I would prove her wrong. I didn't see her for a few months, and in that time I researched all about having a slave, how to be dominant, and the S&M world. This was before the internet, so I had to find special bookshops, going down streets in my town I'd never even found before. It was an eye opener, and a bit scary, but I loved her and wanted to learn how to please her – and, with my teenage bravado, I wanted to prove that I could.

'Then I saw her again, in my new role. She was impressed, and she taught me more and more. She left me anyway; she went to live with a rich old man as his full-time slave, I think. But I realised I loved it as much as she did. I realised that although I love women as friends and lovers and colleagues, I would always seek out this other dynamic too, and that I need to have that in my life. For my first girlfriend, though, it wasn't a game, but a real way of life. She wanted to live it every day, giving herself to someone, not arguing, not complaining, knowing they controlled her. I don't think you would do it. You are moaning about being in the corridor for five minutes. This is a very part-time thing for you.'

He was right. I could never be a 'lifestyle' sub – I am sure much of the excitement for me about occasionally surrendering control is that it is the reverse of my general life, where I am in control of what I am doing. I also wonder if maybe finding a way to lose control in a safe setting is a way of reframing the scary lack-of-control feeling I can get about the world around me when I think about things like politics or climate change. Maybe it's both, but the point is that for me, it's *different* to normality. There is no way I would get off on being told to take the bins out on a Tuesday evening. But as always, I loved to hear about how other people's desires manifested; what a boring world it would be if we all liked the same things.

Francois could clearly get off on the more 24/7 thing. He could have a sub sleep in a cage at the foot of the bed and eat her dinner on the floor. It was the extreme end of immersive; I need breaks after a few hours, and those breaks can sometimes last several months. Anthony and I had discussed this once; he said that if being a dom was constant, it could get boring and perhaps annoying. You'd have to make every single decision about everything, because the person you were with – even if only in pretence – would have no agency. For him, the contrast between a submissive's confident normal personality and their surrendering role was hotter. That kind of full-time dom/sub relationship is even harder for people to understand than the session-based BDSM I play with. But it can exist, and it can be consensual and rewarding, maybe even sublime.

'OK, you have one more question.'

'Er . . . would you like to come on my face?'

'Oh, slut. You are such a slut. You are interrupting our deep conversation by begging for more cum? Fine. You can start by licking all *your* cum off my cock; I can feel how wet you are all over me. You can open your eyes.'

Blinking, I looked at him. Then I moved down his muscular body and started to suck his cock. He stood up and pushed me onto my knees. I looked up and he pulled my hair, fucking my mouth hard. Finally, he pulled out and covered my face and tits in another layer of cum.

He pulled me up. 'You look amazing. Put on your dress – no underwear – and go home.'

I got dressed and said goodbye. He had resumed lying on the bed.

'You show me you want more of this, and we can talk. Goodnight, slut.'

As I walked the short distance to my hotel through deserted business district streets, I noticed I had that odd sense of peace that I often found after submitting. I was no longer so given to intellectually interrogating everything that had happened, so full of curiosity about why and how things had worked. Once, I would have asked myself, *Wow, I really was scared in the corridor, why was that so hot?* These days, I increasingly just accepted that these things *did* work, and that they worked for each of us differently.

All the excitement had wiped the week's anxieties from my brain. I knew I would wake up first thing with a smile on my face. I resolved to write up a blow-by-blow description of the night's events for Max. I wanted to send it to him before I got on my plane, as I knew we'd sit and talk about it when I was back, laughing at the dramatics, him chuckling at the thought of me shivering in the corridor, telling me I was a beautifully odd person. I also knew it would make him extremely horny – and who doesn't want to be welcomed home from a conference with a nice hard cock?

❧

Erika and I both strongly identified with gay male sexual culture. 'I'm a gay man in a woman's body!' is a familiar lament for slutty women; it sounds flippant, but there are serious points.

Erika and I are cis; we both feel that the gender we were assigned at birth is our gender, and we feel comfortable in our bodies. But we both felt from a young age that the sexual roles we were given by society were wrong. Women, whether straight, gay or bi, are supposed to like sex only in the context of deep and meaningful relationships, and with a lot of conversation before (and during, and after).

As a teenager, I loved the sound of gay culture. The clubs, the saunas, the parks, the glory holes: places where you could just look at someone a certain way and immediately fuck. I know that these scenarios were born out of necessity, with homophobic laws and prejudice requiring secrecy and special spaces, but it's brilliant that even now in places where you can have a traditional monogamous marriage, kids and a Volvo as a gay man, the licentious sex spaces have been preserved too.

My oldest school friend, Arno, is gay. His teens, spent at our comprehensive school, were not easy. But when we both moved to London for university, I loved living vicariously through his earliest cruising experiences. I was envious.

Recently, Arno went to a Horse Fair. Participants had to decide in advance whether they were a stable lad, a mare or a stallion – and buy a ticket as such. The mares were to arrive first. They would be taken to the stable lads, who would strip them naked, bind their hands and then cover their heads. The stable lads would then lead the mares to the auction room, where they would be presented to the stallions. The stallions would inspect the bloodstock at their leisure, allowed to feel and touch and assess as required. Once a stallion had picked a mare, he would then lead his mare to the stalls, to use as he wishes. Once he had finished, he would lead the mare back into the auction room and hand him to a stable lad, who would clean him up and get him ready for the next stallion to pick him.

I mean, I could have written that fantasy (though perhaps without muddling up auctions and stud breeding – where is the auction element here? The stallions wouldn't be bidding, surely, but their owners?). Arno had an excellent night, and enjoyed my extreme envy in the recounting.

I think it is extremely unlikely such an event will be publicly held involving women and men any time soon. You could organise your own with people you know, but the risks with strangers might be – or feel – too great. You would sell tickets, I'm sure, but you would be so unlikely to get permission from the authorities, who would assume such an event to be a playground for rapists and a thousand lawsuits waiting to happen. In some ways, it is unfair that men are treated as less vulnerable – male-on-male rape and abuse is just as horrific – but this kind of fantasy-enactment event is so much more common in the gay scene, and doesn't seem to cause the authorities too many headaches.

I don't see why there are not more of these kinds of events for women only, but while there are plenty of socials and parties and general fetish nights, there seem to be very few female-only events that are all about going straight to the sex, without any chat first. Erika tells me that in New York, a group of women are trying to get a female bathhouse scene off the ground, modelled after the gay male spas and saunas. There was a famous Pussy Palace in Toronto, which was a welcoming sauna for people identifying as female. Predictably, during the excellent-sounding '2,000 Pussies' event, it was raided by a swarm of male police officers, who barged in fully clothed to gape at the naked, fucking women, and forced their way into clearly private rooms. The crime? No liquor licence. Perhaps they feared that illegal alcohol sales were taking place under the beds. Once again, the created kink space was safe. The risk and danger came from outside – in this case, from state-sanctioned prejudice, abuse and misunderstanding.

Rape fantasy – or, as it is now more commonly called, 'forced-sex fantasy' – must be one of the thorniest and most controversial of fantasies.

Rape is non-consensual sex. Rape fantasy is consensual. If you have rape fantasies, *this does not mean you want to rape or be raped, nor does it mean that you condone this crime.*

Dr Justin Lehmiller's study in the US found that sixty-three per cent of women and fifty per cent of men (defined by gender assigned at birth) had rape fantasies. It is incredibly common. Academics from many different disciplines are fascinated about why this is, and you can go down an internet rabbit hole exploring various theories. Some suggest that rape fantasy for women is a feminist activity – the idea seems to be that rewriting something that looks similar to rape in our brains, but where we are in fact in control, undoes our legitimate fear of rape in the real world. Some epigeneticists go further and believe that we have collective inherited trauma around rape, and that rape fantasy is about healing it. Some victims of sexual abuse and rape can apparently use rape fantasy as therapy – psychologists report that for some, replaying a narrative but changing it so that they are in charge can heal trauma. However, it seems like this is a rarity in rape fantasy. Nancy Friday suggested that the prevalence of rape fantasy in her collection *My Secret Garden* was to do with the fact that, at that time, women 'wanting' sex was deemed unacceptable, so the 'I was forced against my will' fantasy was a way to mitigate shame in their imaginations. In *Tell Me What You Want*, Dr Lehmiller wonders if it could also be about being the ultimate object of desire – women are culturally told to be desirable sex objects, and the ultimate objectification is being nothing more than a vessel for someone else to use.

Today, psychologists and sex therapists seem to find that role-playing rape fantasy takes place with sexually confident and adventurous people. It feels transgressive, and that is arousing to many people, but it is in fact safe and consensual.

There are as many stages to forced-sex fantasy as any other. There is the unbidden thought that pops into your head as you are masturbating – which, because of the stigma and lack of conversation around fantasy, can make you feel ashamed or anxious, wondering, *Why am I getting off on this?* Then there is deliberate fantasising in your own mind – accepting that it's a narrative which works for you. Maybe there is a sexy talk version, where you co-fantasise with another person in words but not actions, during sex (or indeed over WhatsApp, as you go about your day). Then, if you decide to start role-playing, there is a vast spectrum of ideas to explore, from making use of a simple physical restraint during sex, to an elaborately staged, multi-participant abduction fantasy. I gather Erika, Tom and Max have been planning one of these for me for about five years, but the logistics are so far insurmountable. It involves a van (easy to come by) and an abandoned Gothic church (more complex), and needs to somehow be realistic enough to be incredibly exciting, but also done in a way where I absolutely know I am in a role play and am not being abducted (so far, impossible). Personally, I would reserve the more complicated rape fantasy role plays of this type for people I know extremely well.

As with all fantasies and kinks, if it is one you personally do not respond to, it is so easy to find it repellent.

This is where prejudice comes from. Even if you are not interested in or curious about a particular kink, tolerance and acceptance is surely the answer. Despite the happy explosion of sex positivity on social media, the traditional media (and some parts of social media) still perpetuate the dangerous message that if you fantasise about rape, you are a bad or damaged person. In February 2023, it was announced that actor Gillian Anderson was going to front a new iteration of Nancy Friday's *My Secret Garden*. She invited women to write in with their fantasies, stating:

> I want women across the world, and all of you who identify intrinsically as women now – queer, heterosexual and bisexual, non-binary, transgender, polyamorous – all of you, old and young, whatever your religion, and married, single or other, to write to me and tell me what you think about when you think about sex. Whether it's when you're having it by yourself or with a partner, or with more than one. Tell me. Fantasies, frustrations, explorations, the forbidden, childhood, sounds, fetishes, guilt, insatiability. Fifty years on, the boundaries have been erased, no more so than in our own sexuality: BDSM, the modern meaning of gender, etc. Anything is up for grabs.

But when you decided to send in your innermost fantasy, you would have found that the guidelines on the publisher Bloomsbury's website are specific and strict. For example, your submission may not contain bestiality or 'sexual activity involving sexualised death, rape, abuse, graphic violence, totally unwilling participants, drugging, dangerous sexual acts or mutilation'.

That rules out a large part of Nancy Friday's original seventies collection, which featured bestiality and plenty of forced-sex fantasy, and even a fantasy about sex with a teenage stepson. This attitude speaks to how confused the world is about fantasy. The submissions are supposed to be 'what you *think* about when you *think* about sex'. The publisher's small print might have made people feel that because they do imagine violence as they fantasise, they are too disgusting and ill to be included in a modern collection of fantasy; the opposite to the collection's intended effect.

I suspect that what Bloomsbury really meant was, 'Please do not write in with experiences of when you, in real life, committed an illegal, heinous sex crime.' But to conflate fantasy – by definition consensual – with real-life non-consensual experiences is to entirely miss the point. At the time of writing, the collection is not yet published; it may be that everyone ignored the terms and conditions and the book is a glorious, inclusive celebration of the strange, or even dark, fantasies most of us have – I hope so.

If you want to use any fantasy to inspire an event in real life, the very first question is, 'Can we do this consensually?' Some fantasies can never, ever, be consensual by definition. The Alsatian can never consent. But a happy human furry can, so maybe that's who you might seek out. School-girl fantasies are queasy-making for many, but the school-disco nights out there – and ready availability of 'sexy school-girl' outfits for women to buy online – show it can't be an uncommon fantasy. It involves consenting adults playing what is, to them, sexy dress-up, or maybe exploring a sense of nostalgia for a simpler time in their lives, or reliving their earliest sexual memories.

I love ideas around teacher–student power play, but for me, it's got nothing to do with wearing a fake school tie, while for others, the clothes themselves may be the important or fetishistic thing.

The private fantasies of strangers you will never meet have absolutely no impact upon you. It's amazing that people get so exercised about it. But it comes from this misunderstanding of the chasm of difference between consensual and non-consensual sex-related activity.

As Max and I encountered more people brave enough to open up about their weird and wonderful kinks, I found it fascinating. I don't want to write an academic paper about *why* this person wants to dress in a nappy, or why that person wants to have peanut butter smeared on their anus, but I think it's beautiful if they have found a space to be able to express it without fear of ridicule or judgement.

As I climbed out of the Uber, I was not at all sure what to expect. I was wearing, as directed, my Louboutins, a short black skirt, stockings, an unbuttoned white shirt . . . and no bra or knickers. Unfortunately, even at my most extremely obedient, I am incapable of being on time, and was very aware that I had already broken one clearly stated rule.

I hadn't seen Jordan since before the pandemic. We had been in touch only very intermittently in the years the world was closed, and we both agreed it was time to address this. By now we had been friends for fifteen years, and while he was certainly dominant in a physical way every time we played, and we might have enjoyed some light bondage and spanking, we had never really explored any more elaborate or theatrical kinds of experience together. Jordan, who while living alone must have had quite a lot of time to invent and imagine, was clearly a man with a plan. In fact, the week before our date, he'd told me over text he was no longer Jordan; he was now Master J, and I had to completely submit to his will. I was thrilled at this level of dramatics, and extremely curious about what he had in mind.

Jordan came out to meet me, and it was so nice to see his face after all this time that I couldn't help smiling.

He didn't smile back.

'You're at the wrong gate, and you're late. Walk through there.' He pushed me into the courtyard and I stumbled in my heels. He directed me through a door; there was a corridor and a big industrial goods lift. I stopped, waiting for direction.

'Choose.'

I went for the corridor, as this seemed more likely.

'Wrong!' he said, exasperated. I had the sense he was tallying my misdemeanours.

He yanked opened the wide metal concertina door with a force that made me shiver in nervous anticipation. He pushed me into the big lift, pulled the door shut behind us and sent the lift up. He grabbed me, and pushed me up against the wall of the lift, crushing my face hard into the metal. He spread my legs, and slapped me between them, very hard. I shouted out. He slapped me again, a few more times. I was suddenly extremely present.

He pulled me up and tied a scarf around my eyes. I heard him grind open the industrial lift door, and then he pushed me out in front of him. I was stumbling, blind and in high heels. I heard him open a door, and he tumbled me inside. I fell against metal; maybe it was a cupboard. He grasped my arms behind me, and cuffed my hands with tight metal cuffs. They cut into my wrists. Then I heard the clang of chains. I felt heavy metal being looped around my neck and arms, then clanking against something else. I wriggled, and knew I was tied up to something. He pushed me against the wall, slapping my arse and my face. He suddenly looped his arms through my legs and lifted me high into the air. *Fuck me*, I thought, *you are strong*.

My skin was tingling, and my cunt was already sore from being slapped and wet from having fingers roughly pushed inside it, and from feeling his cock pressed against me – deliberately, I well knew. He told me he was going to get drinks; he could be any length of time. I was tied up, and couldn't move more than a few centimetres. He turned off the light – it became even darker under my blindfold – and I heard him lock the door on the way out.

I tried to wriggle to get a bit more comfortable. It didn't work; metal was pinching my skin, and I was standing at an awkward, leg-numbing angle. As I waited in the dark, shivering in delicious fear, I thought to myself that this was really *quite* an intense opening gambit – what could Jordan possibly have in store? The cuffs cut into my wrists and the chains were cold against my skin. I couldn't see anything, or move. I wondered, once again, what could possibly have gone wrong in my brain for me to be so wet at this kind of scenario . . . but at the same time, I was also chuckling in delight at having been plunged into such an artistic theatrical production. I love that even people you have known for ever can surprise you.

What felt like hours passed, during which my limbs were cramping and my cunt was getting wetter and wetter with all the possibilities running through my mind. At the same time, I was getting pretty scared that someone else would somehow find me, or that Jordan had been run over and I would be stuck here for ever. But then he returned, and unlocked the door of the store cupboard, or whatever it was. He untied the chains from where they had been secured, and looped them around my neck, heavy and cold. He pushed me in front of him, still blindfolded and handcuffed. I stumbled as he directed me through a door.

'Welcome to my church,' he said.

Gospel music was playing.

He pushed me onto a seat and spread my legs. I could hear him moving around, and the sound of his iPhone taking photos – presumably, he had deliberately not silenced the camera's shutter sound so I would know he was taking pictures of me in such a humiliating situation.

He finally removed the blindfold, and I looked around at his warehouse. There were ominous-looking objects arranged around the space and a hook in the ceiling.

'Now,' he said, 'you know my name. Or you think you know my name. But that is my slave name. You think you are one of those woke liberals. You don't know anything. And you think you are some literary genius. So I thought it would be fun to do some reading.'

Fucking hell, I thought, *where is THIS going?* As a white, 'woke liberal', I had always been extremely squeamish about race play, common as it seemingly is as a fantasy. Jordan is Black, but he had never as much as referred to his 'black cock' in the time we had known each other. Over the years, a few other Black men had worked their race into play or chat in some way with me, and if they were getting off on it, I didn't object. I had been curious but hadn't felt comfortable enough with anyone to ask more about what race-related kink was doing for them – especially at a time when conversations in real life around race were so charged.

'You may have read a lot of books, but I don't think you have read this one.' He placed a chair in front of me, and put on top of it a copy of *The Making of a Slave* by Willie Lynch.

I felt extremely uncomfortable and a little bit sick. Was he going to make me act out, and then no doubt get turned on by, horrific, real, historical plantation practices? Would I then actually die of shame? Are there any submissives in the world who have not felt ashamed that they might have accidentally borrowed their fantasies from the most heinous real-life events? Is this the ultimate white privilege? I mean, it's bad enough to be perennially turned on by what looks externally like a parody of domestic abuse and rape, without real-life slavery being added to the mix. So, Jordan had succeeded already in making me feel humiliated and ashamed of my desires, and also quite scared.

He uncuffed my hands and placed the toxic-looking book into them. Paragraphs had been highlighted. I had to read them aloud. Whenever I stumbled over a word or stopped, he would add to the tally of marks against me.

When I first encountered the N-word, I said, 'I'm not saying that!'

'Keep reading,' he said. 'I am going to film you.'

I felt quite panicked. The content of the text was extremely dark, as you would expect.

'You are going to call me Master N----- from now on.'

'Agghhh,' I said.

'Say it!'

It was possibly the first time I had ever thought about calling it in the middle of an elaborately planned role play, but somehow my desire to submit to him, whatever he wanted me to do, took over.

I mumbled the name.

'Ha,' he said. 'Soon, you won't have any problem with it.'

Finally, I was allowed to stop reading and he released me from the chair. He made me crawl over to a different section of the warehouse on my hands and knees. There, he lay me backwards over a stool, and I flinched as he lifted his hand.

He laughed. 'That's enough for me. What do you say?'

'Er . . . thank you, er . . . Master J.'

'Master what?' He slapped me.

'Ahh, Master N-----,' I whispered.

'See, you're getting the hang of it.'

Pushing me onto my knees he took out his cock. He slapped my face with it. Then he pushed it deep into my throat till I choked and gagged. I couldn't help but imagine him pushing it into my cunt with the same force.

We went back to the other side of the warehouse. He presented me with another book, which was called

The Encyclopaedia of Unusual Sex Practices. I read some highlighted sections aloud. It was quite funny, and really interesting. I suspect Jordan could see I was not sufficiently terrified by this book – indeed, reading about weird and wonderful kinks was a lovely reprieve from the last book – so soon enough, I was turned around and bending over a table. I saw him take a metal fish slice from the kitchen. He whipped me with it until I was crying out and there were tears in my eyes. Then he pushed it between my arse cheeks and told me to hold it there.

Soon, something was being pushed into my arse. I was wincing, and he was laughing, at how tight it was and how that wasn't going to matter to him. He fucked me everywhere with an elaborate combination of dildos, vibrators and his cock, until I was coming again and again, and felt like purple bruises were forming in every orifice.

Eventually, I was allowed to have a rest. When he released me, I had that euphoric rush of love and lust and relief, and just wanted to curl up in his stupidly strong arms. Master J became Jordan again, and we had some wine and sat on the sofa.

'Well, you're completely crazy,' I said. 'You know, in a good way.'

When we felt a bit revived, I asked him to talk to me about the race element he had introduced, if he was happy to. I love having these post-session conversations with partners I have known for a long time; it means that we can talk about things, safe in the knowledge that it won't harm our relationship. It's as if our play – which is so intimate – creates a beautiful space for emotional intimacy too.

Jordan said that living alone through Covid had given him a lot of time and space to think, and work through various things. Black Lives Matter and the conversation around race had made him think about his identity more. He was adopted as a baby by a white middle-class family, and had what he'd always considered to be a normal and relatively privileged childhood. But he had come to realise that this scenario had left him with a strange split identity – not feeling properly Black, because his family were white, but still absolutely being subjected to all the prejudice directed at Black men, because of how he looked. His industry is extremely white. He was so used to being the only person of colour in a room that it had felt normal, but he had recently been seeing that, in fact, all this racism had taken a personal toll. He started reading more about slavery and race, trying to come to terms with it all – an enormous, impossible task. He sounded like he was battling with feelings of anger and trauma conflicting with the sense that 'so many Black people have it worse'.

I don't think he had consciously thought that playing with historically racist texts and concepts in a kink setting would be healing for him. The idea had come to him seemingly randomly, as fantasies do, and he'd thought it was hot. He liked the subversion of him as a master and a white person bound in chains, rewriting history. Psychologists say that this is not uncommon – and, indeed, mentally rewriting troubling or traumatic stories in our heads, fantasising better outcomes, is a psychological technique taught by therapists.

Also, though – and here he grinned mischievously – he'd known that I would *hate* it, and he thought I was getting too blasé about all the normal BDSM games. He wanted to see me properly uncomfortable and scared, like I would have been when faced with a small flogger when we'd first met.

We chatted more, ate some biscuits, got into bed and spooned lazily, until we got over excited and energetic again. I went home on an early-morning Tube, feeling lighter than air.

❧

Max had decided that maybe the ultimate expression of the 'make anonymous people fuck Sonnet' theme was to make a profile for me on a sex-worker website, and pimp me out to paying men. This felt like a new level of submission. There was an extra level of fear and danger in meeting people who were not from the kink or swinging universes. There was a sense of humiliation in being paid for sex, even though I really don't think that it is or should be humiliating in real life. There was a certain role-playing joy in having to pretend to be someone else – although, when I thought about it, if you were being paid to fuck someone, and then you did fuck them, you *were* a sex worker, not play-acting at being one. Indeed, to this day, I have to tick the 'have you ever been paid for sex?' box at the STI clinic, which really gets you screened for *everything*.

Max knew it was going to push me out of my comfort zone in new and delicious ways.

I got very nervous about the logistics. When do you ask for money? How much small talk is there before you start fucking? What do you wear? Who are the clients?

People are forced into trading sex for money for someone else the world over. This is slavery, not work. The unimaginably horrifying fact that slavery exists does not mean that sex work cannot be positive for both clients and providers in completely different contexts. I used to feel very judgemental about people who attended sex parties with a paid partner – and, indeed, at some parties I attended in my twenties, there were definitely bad vibes where it was clear a man had only paid a young, beautiful female sex worker to come with him because single men were not allowed, especially as he often then ignored her and was voyeuristic and unpleasant to other women at the party. However, if you wanted to go to a kink night as a sub and be led around as a slave, and you paid a professional dominatrix for this, then why not? You are still participating properly in the event. I learned from the pro-doms I occasionally met at these nights that just because money has changed hands, it doesn't mean the experience can't feel as real and as sublime as my amateur encounters. And, just as in my BDSM adventures, it can also sometimes be boring, hard work or lacking in connection.

When the first client came round to our flat, Max hid in another room. I was shaking with nerves as I let in a young man who was even more nervous than me. It turned out he was a refugee and had fled horrendous persecution, abandoning his family and everything he knew. All his friends and family were either dead or scattered across the globe. He had managed, somehow, to get a student visa and was studying in London, but he wasn't making connections and friends, and he was exhausted. I suspected he was also suffering from extreme PTSD.

He opened up about all this quite quickly. I wondered if 'proper' sex workers would have somehow started having sex and not just sat listening like an extremely unqualified therapist. Later, talking to sex workers, I found that clients opening up like this is common; one woman I know sometimes calls herself a 'sex nurse' because of the healing nature of the service she is offering. She has all sorts of clients, including many you might not imagine: straight women who want to try bondage but are too afraid to be tied up by men; people with cancer who need respite from pain and anxiety; people who see her weekly as they would a counsellor, and talk as much as they fuck; as well as people who, because of the transactional nature of the experience, simply feel they can ask for things they need that they just couldn't ask for from their partners or dates.

My client started crying, and I just held him for a while. I asked what he wanted to do, and he wanted to lie naked, quietly. So we did. I put on some music and gently undressed us both, and then we lay entwined on the bed. It seemed that on top of everything else he had been through, loneliness is partly a very physical thing about lack of skin contact with other people. It's not necessarily even about sexual contact – I have one friend who decided to be single and celibate for a year, and she realised she had to book weekly massages to remain tethered to people and connection. Social media just can't replace skin.

I didn't take any money. I offered to stay in touch as a friend, and Max determined to screen potential clients a bit more closely in terms of what they were after, with the aim of making my experience of being submissive more fun. But although it wasn't exactly what we'd been planning, I realised I would never have come across this man in any other context. My life was richer for having met him, and I hoped his was made even momentarily better thanks to an hour of physical touch.

I met a few other clients, from a straight couple who wanted to have a threesome to a City boy who wanted a relaxing lunchtime quickie. The problem was, as a submission to Max, it worked in advance and afterwards, as I had to hand over my earnings to my pimp – even if he immediately spent it on dinner for us – but it didn't work for me in the sessions themselves. The clients were genuinely paying for a service which I wanted to give to them. I was very far away from my submissive role in these sessions; if anything, I felt like it was my responsibility to direct proceedings. As a BDSM activity, a better version was when the supposed client was in the know too; even if he was a stranger to me, I knew he had been recruited to dominate his whore in all sorts of deviant ways because he had paid for the privilege. And her pimp might even show up and join in.

Still, I was happy to have had this tiny insight into the world of sex work, and to see yet another way in which humans find solace in touch.

Max and I were on holiday in Spain. We had rented a tumbledown cottage for a week on a remote clifftop. It had no aircon or Wi-Fi, a single gas hob and a rusty old barbecue outside. It was beautiful.

It was a scorching July, and every morning we woke early, our sweaty limbs entangled. We would be fucking before we were properly awake. I slept wearing an eye mask, as the morning light was so bright. Sometimes I would feel Max before I could see him, as he pushed his fingers into my cunt. I would reach up to remove the mask, and he would grab my wrist and pin me down, put his cock in me, and fuck me while I was still blind. It was an excellent way to wake up, feeling every other sense first, before sight. The first communication of the day being purely touch.

I loved how, after thirteen years together, we didn't need to have a conversation about this kind of thing. Max knows that is how I would like to wake up on pretty much any day, but certainly on a lovely holiday morning with no breakfast meetings or spin classes to worry about.

We would then make coffee and get back into bed, opening the door to the cabin to let in the air and the stray cats. The sun on our limbs would make us horny again, and with caffeinated energy, Max would flip me onto all fours and I'd grab the creaky headboard in happiness.

There were secluded secret beaches all around, and we would hike to a different one each day, scrambling down the rocks and, delighted to find no one else there, immediately stripping and streaking into the sea. We sunbathed naked, and sent selfies to our kinky WhatsApp groups, imagining what we could get up to with a group of deviant perverts on such a beach. There were some official nudist beaches in the area, which were slightly more popular. Every time someone walked past us lying on our backs on our towels, Max would subtly pull my thighs apart, exposing my cunt to them. Feeling the hot Mediterranean sun on it was as arousing as the thought of strangers seeing it. I wondered what it would feel like to get sunburned on your labia. One day, we realised we must be on a cruising beach, as we saw men parade naked up and down the shoreline, meet each other, then head behind some rocks. They seemed unconcerned by our presence, and all the sex clearly going on around us made us rush for our own secluded dune to frolic in.

In the evenings, we would barbecue fish and sit outside under the stars, revelling in a temperature that required so very few clothes.

After the most relaxing of weeks, we headed to Barcelona for a couple of nights before flying home. We were wandering around the city, noticing hot people everywhere. Being back in a metropolis made us feel sociable again.

'Shall we see if there's anyone about?' asked Max, and I nodded.

We stopped for a beer and had a look at Feeld. Things were so much easier now in the world of smartphones that work everywhere and apps that function in every country. Feeld started life as 'Thrinder', specifically billed as 'Tinder for threesomes'. After its rebrand, it was more encompassing and much broader. It was almost easier to define it as *not* being just for finding a life partner, rather than trying to pin down what it *was* for. I had monogamous heterosexual friends using it to find no-strings sex when they weren't up for relationships, while others used it to find partners for extreme BDSM play. There were always lots of couples looking for other couples, and, of course, lots of creepy single men who couldn't spell, their pictures wonky torsos only, seemingly taken in a pub toilet. The only downside of Feeld these days is that now *everyone* is on it, which makes it harder to keep a kink life secret – you know your colleague has probably scrolled past your profile and discovered you're in an open relationship and like to be pissed on.

Max was still in charge of all things internet. This was out of necessity, as I would never remember to check the inbox and found all the scrolling intensely tedious, whereas he seemed to find it as addictive as social media. He opened the app, and we started to browse through the perverts currently available in Barcelona. There were people from all over the world, wanting to do all sorts of things. We matched with a cute Brazilian couple who were online, and we exchanged some messages, but sadly they were only free the next day, when we had to return home. We found a girl who wanted to be placed in a hotel room as if she was furniture, then ignored. This tickled us, but we decided we were hungry to touch and play with other bodies, not just fuck in front of someone pretending to be a standing lamp.

Then we found Sven. He had a nice profile, he looked hot – athletic and tall – in his pictures, and the text was well-written. He described himself as a 'bull-dom', which can mean various things, but implies extreme dominance. In cuckolding play, the 'bull' is the one doing the cuckolding – i.e., fucking the wife while the husband watches. There are also connotations of being well-endowed, which seemed to be apt in this instance, as he noted right at the bottom of his profile that he sported ten and a half inches. He stated he was bisexual, interested in all combinations of people, and hosted parties. He even included an excellent mini-essay on consent. He seemed experienced and articulate.

Max messaged him, and he got right back and said he was around. We switched to WhatsApp and had a chat about what we were into. Max said he loved to watch me being brutally used by another man, rightly surmising Sven might be into that. Sven asked if Max was bi too; Max replied he presented as straight, but wasn't against sucking a nice cock if the situation required. Sven asked if I would like to be DP-ed – double-penetrated – obviously a yes, and how I felt about pain, to which Max prevented me from writing an academic paper-length reply. Sven sent kinky pictures of himself at fun-looking parties, and we did the same. With these preliminaries out of the way, and all of us reassured we were on the same page, he asked if we were free now. He was only about twenty minutes away; he said he was out walking his dogs, and we could meet him in the park. Before we set off, Max told me to go to the toilets and take off my bra and knickers. I was wearing a white linen strappy sundress, which was quite sheer. I did as he said, and noted in the mirror that you could definitely see my nipples. I came back out, and Max nodded in approval.

We spotted Sven strolling around with two little dogs, Pomeranian-Chihuahua crosses, so hilariously incongruous for a very tall, broad bull-dom German. But we were used to the vast chasms of difference between people's kinks and their day-to-day personalities, and were not surprised to find Sven to be laidback, wearing shorts and a T-shirt, and clearly a devoted parent to two fluffy canine princesses.

He suggested a drink at a little café bar, and we got some small beers. He was from Berlin, where he had been a stalwart of the thriving kink scene, but had relocated to Barcelona for the sun and the beaches. He was a digital nomad who spent his spare time surfing and getting up to kinky fun with locals and the many visiting tourists. We told him a bit about ourselves. As we all chatted about the kinds of things we had done and enjoyed, I could feel my cunt getting wetter. I was sitting between Max and Sven. Max reached down and opened my knees, pulling up my dress to show my cunt to Sven. Sven pointedly looked down and stared. I love that moment where normal chat becomes play, and everyone switches into gear and starts falling into their roles. It's now so familiar, my physical response so automatic, like the opening theme tune to a favourite TV show making you feel immediately relaxed.

Sven stroked my thigh, and looked at Max. 'Should we take her back to my flat?'

When we arrived, he took us through to the kitchen to give the dogs some water and offer us drinks. As he did this, Max pulled my dress off over my head. Sven looked me up and down, and nodded approvingly. He pulled me in and kissed me. I pressed against him and felt his cock harden. Max came up behind me and pressed into my arse. That feeling of being naked and vulnerable to two clothed men: it will never, ever get old. The tinge of exhibitionism, the feeling of being slutty and showing it, them knowing how much you want them, how much you want to be fucked, and the certainty it will happen very soon.

They led me into the bedroom. Max asked Sven if he minded if he took some photos; of course, they wouldn't be shared. Sven was fine with it. Max went to get his film camera. Sven took out his cock with a palpable sense of pride, which I immediately thought was highly justified. It was very long, but not so very broad, which made me excited to deep-throat. As Max came back, I was on my knees with tears in my eyes as Sven fucked my mouth. I caught Max's eye and he smiled down at me, as if to say, *Oh, look, you found your happy place*. Sven pulled me up and threw me onto the bed, then Max opened my thighs and pressed them down with his hands. Sven put his fingers in my cunt and laughed at how wet it was. 'Oh, you are so ready for me already.'

He grabbed a condom and I watched him unroll it down the long shaft. As he eased into me, he said, 'It's going to be hard and deep and fast.' He looked at me seriously. 'You have to say if it's too much, OK?'

I nodded, deliciously nervous. Max held me down as he began to pound into me, all his weight bearing down into me through his cock. Max undressed and climbed onto the bed over my head. Sven looked at his cock approvingly: 'Nice cock, Max.' Max began to fuck my mouth. Sven could feel my cunt squeeze every time Max choked me, and Max could feel my throat constrict every time my cunt spasmed thanks to Sven. I loved being a sensory conduit between them.

We were all quickly drenched in sweat. Sven pulled out and wiped his brow, and lay down next to me on the bed. 'Fuck, this is so hot, in all ways.'

He started to fuck me with his fingers. First a couple, then four, and then his whole hand. Harder and harder, my G-spot swelling and my body spasming, my legs having a twitchy life of their own. He was unrelenting. I was groaning and gasping, the pain – and such an internal kind of pain – mingling so well with the pleasure. Max put his hands around my neck to choke me at the same time. Sven didn't care if I came; he didn't stop when I did. He just kept on wrenching into me with his strong hands, as deeply as he could. Eventually, he decided I had had enough.

We all lay back and gulped down water.

'When did you find out you liked that?' he asked.

I thought about it, but I couldn't remember. My brain was fizzing, and I couldn't really think about much except the heat inside my cunt.

We relaxed for a while.

'I think it's time for you to take us both. I've stretched you nice and open,' said Sven.

He lay back on the bed and I straddled him. I held my cunt open with my hands as Max knelt behind me. Their cocks rubbed against each other as they both tried to squeeze in. I breathed deeply, willing my muscles to become liquid, to submit to both of them. For a brief moment, they were both deep inside. I felt like I was being cracked open from within, like that bit in *The Fifth Element* where a giant beam of light breaks out of Milla Jovovich's chest. But quickly my cunt spasmed of its own accord and pushed Max out. We all laughed and flopped back.

'We need a swing, really,' said Sven, with endearing Germanic practicality. 'I think I'm going to build one in the spare room.'

'I'm getting kind of hungry,' said Max, as Sven went to the kitchen. 'You up for leaving soon?'

With Max's general need to eat a multi-course meal every couple of hours, this was probably the legitimate reason, but our agreement, long since unspoken, was that when one of us is ready to leave, we leave. We told Sven we were going to head off, and to look us up when he was next in London. We all hugged goodbye.

Max and I popped back to the hotel for a much-needed shower, then went out to dinner somewhere we had been recommended, enjoying small plates and orange wine. We talked about how, although the world was quite fucked in many obvious ways, hooking up for mid-afternoon threesomes in a foreign city had definitely become easier. I wondered, though, if it wasn't just because of the technology. It simply seemed easier for us these days than it had when we were first together. 'Casual sex' is the wrong word for something that feels so big in the moment; it's transcendental, sensory and a lot of fun. The phrase gives the hilariously inaccurate idea that sex in monogamous relationships is less casual than the sex you have with people with whom you have met up with specifically for something intense and beautiful.

The truth was that meeting up with a fun stranger was just *not a big deal* anymore. In fact, I mused, maybe it was easier to enjoy all the activities and sensations precisely *because* it didn't feel like a particularly unusual activity, something out-there or deviant. For us, and many, many others, it had become quite normal. It wasn't something we needed to talk through with each other in detail anymore; we each had the confidence to say what we wanted and the ability to read the situation – and to leave when we fancied tapas by ourselves. For the millionth time, we told each other how grateful we were to have found a partner who wanted to live like this. I love Max for so many reasons, and in so many ways, but part of it is certainly how he encourages me to celebrate my innately kinky and slutty self, and how good that makes me feel.

We went back to work tanned and refreshed, and when people asked about our holiday, we said it had been excellent, and did not elaborate.

I had come to learn that I loved the really immersive scenarios: strange settings, a strong sense of mystery and drama, even unease. A long set-up, a day or weekend put aside. These only worked with people I knew well, and people who loved to devote their energies to their creation.

Humans are innately creative; we all need creativity in our lives. There are countless classic self-help books that tell us how to find it, from Julia Cameron's *The Artist's Way* to *Big Magic* by Elizabeth Gilbert. None of them mention that directing elaborate BDSM sessions might satisfy those desires for authorial omnipotence, but I think it is implied. In *Big Magic*, Elizabeth Gilbert talks about how creative ideas are floating around the universe waiting to find the right mouthpiece, and how we can make ourselves open to receiving them. I loved looking at this thought in terms of kink; maybe we all put our fantasies out into the ether, and then they alight on the appropriate playwright, who will bring them to the stage.

Fortunately for me, Max, Jordan, Anthony, Tom and Erika, among others, loved to direct and produce, and knew that they could rely on my committed method acting.

By chance, Anthony and I were both working in LA one spring. We had met up a few times for various sessions, and he had presented me with a new cane he had bought from a dungeon in Silver Lake. My inner thighs were delightfully stripy. He had established I was free for the weekend, and told me we were taking a trip.

He collected me from Venice Beach in the morning, in a convertible white Mustang with the top down. The Californian winter sun was beginning to burn off the early-morning clouds, and it looked like a beautiful day for a road trip. I climbed into the front seat, wearing a bikini top and short denim cut-offs, which exposed all the bruises on my inner thighs. Of course, I had no knickers on under the shorts. Anthony stroked the bruises and then slapped my inner thigh hard, which was excruciating on the delicate skin there.

We drove out of the city, and soon the skyscrapers were making way for flat scrubland, while mountains rose up against the horizon. There was already a very Wild West, lawless feel to the landscape, even this close to the city. We drove onto the freeway and soon we were leaving civilisation behind. We got to Barstow – the place where 'the drugs began to take hold' in *Fear and Loathing in Las Vegas*. It's on the edge of the desert. Originally on the wagon trail and then later a Gold Rush town, it's always been a stopping point for travellers.

Anthony turned off the freeway and told me to take off my shorts, then drove down a lane to the original Route 66 road, which has been disused since they built the freeway. He pulled over and told me to get out of the car and walk into the scrubland. I did so. He followed and, after a few metres, told me to get on my hands and knees, in amongst the spiky bushes. There was a big crack, and I felt a searing pain. I looked up. Anthony had found a large branch with several off-shoots; it was stiff, and covered in little spikes. He proceeded to flog my arse with it several times, while I screeched out and dug my nails into the stony ground. Then he made me walk back to the car. There was a woman walking along the road who possibly saw all of this, but Barstow seems like such a strange frontier town, they've probably seen it all before.

We had lunch at Jenny's Grill Steak and Mariscos, and a beer helped me calm down and forget my stinging arse. Then we set off once more, through the mountain roads and into the Mojave Desert. The scenery was stunning, the completely flat desert dramatically punctuated by stark, pointed mountains. There was a palpable sense that if you pulled off the road, you would be completely alone in this vast, inhospitable wilderness. When we had left Barstow long behind and driven up and through a couple of the mountain ranges, Anthony abruptly pulled off the freeway and started to drive down a road heading into the desert. I did not ask any questions. He turned off the road, and followed some tyre tracks in the sand out into the wilderness. He stopped the car in a clearing, surrounded by spiky shrubs and cacti. He told me to get out of the car and strip completely. I did so. He took his camera from the car and grabbed my wrist, then strode off across the sand, with me stumbling along over the little stones in my bare feet.

After a few metres, he said, 'Hands and knees.'

I knelt down in the sand. Anthony circled around and took a picture. Then he came back, having found another spiky stick. He dragged the stick over my body and then raised it up, bringing it down hard on my bottom. I screamed; I could feel all the little spikes on top of the force of the main branch. I writhed around in pain, and I could feel his impatience as I tried to collect myself and thank him. He gave me another couple of strokes. Then he sighed and said since I couldn't stay still, I had to lie down flat. I lay fully face down in the sand and dirt. He said my legs were not wide apart enough, and roughly kicked each leg out. I could feel my cunt, exposed to the sun and the wind. Anthony pushed his fingers into it and, presumably finding it wet, smeared his fingers around the lips in a way that made me feel like a photographic prop being prepared. He walked around and took some photos, in silence.

I felt very exposed and helpless. I couldn't see what he was doing, as my face was in the sand – and then I stopped hearing his footsteps. I tried not to look up at first, but curiosity got the better of me, and eventually I lifted my head enough to see that he had walked back to the car. In that instant, I completely believed he was going to drive away and leave me lying naked in the middle of the desert.

I felt a rising tide of panic and fear, and my heart began to race, but there was nothing at all I could do. So I pressed my face back into the sand and tried to stay still, concentrating on how nice the sun felt on my back and on my tingling buttocks. It felt like the skin there was broken, but I wasn't sure.

Eventually, I heard Anthony's feet approach, and was so relieved and grateful. I did not look up. He walked right up to my head, and then I saw a stream of piss just next to my face. I tried to stay still as he pissed right next to me, droplets bouncing off the dry earth onto my cheek. When he was finished, he told me to get up and go back to the car. I scrambled to my feet and walked back while he followed me. I was covered in dirt and sand.

We got into the car and drove back towards the freeway. I picked up my shorts.

'Did I tell you to put your clothes on?'

I shook my head, but said that it was cold, and the road was heading back up into the mountains, where the air would be even cooler.

He said, 'So what?'

I nodded and leaned back in the car seat, letting the cold air brush over my skin. I watched the wind lift the dirt from my goose-pimpled stomach, and felt at peace. I felt at one with the inhospitable, expansive landscape around us, wild and free, far from petty human conventions and the inconsequential, anxious minutiae of ordinary modern life. I was a 'bare fork'd animal', we all are, and daring to show that to another person – that is sublime.

A quote from *Fear and Loathing in Las Vegas* played through my mind:

> No sympathy for the devil; keep that in mind. Buy the ticket, take the ride . . . and if it occasionally gets a little heavier than what you had in mind, well . . . maybe chalk it up to forced consciousness expansion: Tune in, freak out, get beaten.

'Forced consciousness expansion' – what a great way of putting it. I smiled to myself.

Anthony looked over. 'Are you thinking about Hunter S. Thompson?'

I chuckled in surprise. Then shrugged. 'This is bat country.'

He laughed, and we drove along the empty, dusty road in companionable silence.

After a couple of hours, the sun began to set over the mountains – red, purple, yellow – like perfect bruises on soft, willing skin. Vegas rose up out of the desert in front of us, the windows of all the hotels catching the last rays and glinting. Unreal city.

I submitted completely to the adventure.

Acknowledgements

I'm sure writing any book must be a strange and scary thing, but a secret sex memoir has its own special complexities, and there is no way I could have done it without the vast empathy and support of many people.

My agent Lucy Luck – officially the sexiest name in publishing – somehow understood how my diaries could be a book, and who might want to publish them. I'm not sure she knew quite how much oversharing this was going to entail, and how all her emails would now be forever quarantined so her corporate overlords can check them for pornographic content, but she is the best champion and protector anyone could have.

Thank you to incredible C&W rights director Kate Burton and her team, César Castañeda Gámez, Polly Pereza-Brown and Sam Downs – I am so tickled by imagining you at international book fairs describing BDSM scenes to unsuspecting editors from all over the world.

My editor Harriet Poland – I could never have expected the early material to have met with such delighted and wild enthusiasm, followed by nuanced, thoughtful and compassionate editing. The editorial comment 'more cock here' is life advice I am taking very seriously. One day I am throwing you a massive Georgian England-themed immersive sex party in thanks.

A huge thank you to everyone at Hodder: publisher Hannah Black for being forever calm and supportive, publicist extraordinaire Becca Mundy, and editor Tom Atkins, especially for your eagle-eyed continuity comments – 'wouldn't you still be covered in piss?'. And to big boss lady Katie Espiner, who should definitely become a pro-dom if the whole running a publishing empire thing gets boring.

In the US, Maddie Caldwell at Grand Central is the smartest, kindest, unshockable – and most fun – editor you could meet. And thanks to publicist Stef Acquaviva, marketeer Theresa DeLucci and assistant Morgan Spehar, for so passionately taking on the task of persuading the USA they need to read about kink.

Thank you to all the participants in the book who reacted so positively to being featured in print – and indeed, to everyone not in it. All of you constantly give me so much joy, reflection and beautiful bruises. Especial thanks to Anthony – it was an honour to hear your side of the story too, and to spend so much more time walking up your stone steps, creating some next-level content for a sequel. And to Tom and Erika, for all your thoughts, early reads, wisdom, friendship and… next-level fucking. And for hosting the weirdest secret book launch the world will likely ever see.

Thank you to generous early readers, authors Keiran Goddard and Marianne Power – both your comments meant so much.

Thank you to my other friends in the know, for being there through the very strange process of writing anonymously about your sex life, with acceptance and discretion.

Most of all, thank you to Max. May the day never come when you stop saying, 'So I have found this person who wants to do this thing to you, I think you should try it…' Here's to being slutty deviants for as long as we live.